PARALLEL COMPUTING

PARALLEL COMPUTING

An Introduction

by

**Edward L. Lafferty
Marion C. Michaud
Myra Jean Prelle
Joann B. Goethert**

The MITRE Corporation
Bedford, Massachusetts

NOYES DATA CORPORATION
Park Ridge, New Jersey, U.S.A.

Copyright © 1993 by Noyes Data Corporation
Library of Congress Catalog Card Number: 93-866
ISBN: 0-8155-1329-1

Published in the United States of America by
Noyes Data Corporation
Mill Road, Park Ridge, New Jersey 07656

Transferred to Digital Printing, 2011

Printed and bound in the United Kingdom

Library of Congress Cataloging-in-Publication Data

Parallel computing : an introduction / by Edward L. Lafferty . . . [et
    al.].
            p.   cm.
        Includes bibliographical references (p.   ) and index.
        ISBN 0-8155-1329-1
        1. Parallel processing (Electronic computers) 2. Parallel
    computers. I. Lafferty, Edward L.
    QA76.58.P3756   1993
    004'.35--dc20
                                            93-866
                                            CIP

Foreword

Today's supercomputers and parallel computers provide an unprecedented amount of computational power in one machine. A basic understanding of the parallel computing techniques that assist in the capture and utilization of that computational power is essential to appreciate the capabilities and the limitations of parallel supercomputers. In addition, an understanding of technical vocabulary is critical in order to discuss parallel computers. The relevant techniques, vocabulary, currently available hardware architectures, and programming languages which provide the basic concepts of parallel computing are introduced in this book.

The information in the book is from *Introduction to Parallel Computing,* prepared by E.L. Lafferty, M.C. Michaud, M.J. Prelle, and J.B. Goethert of the MITRE Corporation, issued May 1992.

The table of contents is organized in such a way as to serve as a subject index and provides easy access to the information contained in the book.

Advanced composition and production methods developed by Noyes Data Corporation are employed to bring this durably bound book to you in a minimum of time. Special techniques are used to close the gap between "manuscript" and "completed book." In order to keep the price of the book to a reasonable level, it has been partially reproduced by photo-offset directly from the original report and the cost saving passed on to the reader. Due to this method of publishing, certain portions of the book may be less legible than desired.

About the Authors

Edward L. Lafferty is a MITRE Fellow and Chief Engineer in the Center for Integrated Intelligence Systems at The MITRE Corporation in Bedford, Massachusetts.

Marion C. Michaud is a Group Leader in the Intelligence Systems Integration Department at The MITRE Corporation at the San Antonio, Texas site.

Myra Jean Prelle is a Principal Scientist in the National Intelligence Division at The MITRE Corporation in Bedford, Massachusetts.

Joann B. Goethert is a former employee of The MITRE Corporation. She was a Technical Assistant in the Ground–Based Department at the Rome, New York site.

Acknowledgments

We gratefully acknowledge and thank E.H. Bensley, T.J. Brando, E.L. Lafferty, M.J. Prelle, R.D. Silverman, and S.J. Stuart, authors of "Introduction to Parallel Supercomputing," [Bensley:88a], and "Parallel Supercomputing—A Tutorial and Survey," for the organization, information, and paragraphs which were used in part and in whole in this document.

We also wish to thank E.H. Bensley for writing section 2.5, *Parallelism Within Processors*, P.C. Barr for his input on data flow languages, D.E. Emery for his expert wealth of knowledge on Ada, and R.T. Hammel and J.G. Scarano for sharing their experience using Linda. In addition, we thank staff throughout MITRE who gave time and returned phone calls regarding their experience with the machines and languages mentioned in this document. We would also like to thank M.H. Cheheyl for helpful comments on the document as a whole.

All products are trademarks of their respective companies.

Notice

To the best of our knowledge the information in this
publication is accurate; however, the authors and the Publisher
do not assume any responsibility or liability for the accuracy
or completeness of, or consequences arising from use of such
information. Mention of trade names or commercial products
does not constitute endorsement or recommendation for use by
the authors or the Publisher.

Final determination of the suitability of any information or
product for use contemplated by any user, and the manner of
that use, is the sole responsibility of the user. We recommend
that anyone intending to rely on any recommendation of
materials or procedures for parallel computing mentioned in
this publication should satisfy himself as to such suitability,
and that he can meet all applicable safety and health standards.

The MITRE Corporation will retain a non–exclusive royalty–
free license throughout the world in each invention that has
been disclosed to the Government as a result of the work
performed during the conduct of the contract which was the
result of the data being used herein.

Contents and Subject Index

SECTION 1

INTRODUCTION

It is appropriate to begin with a discussion of supercomputers. Supercomputers provide the ultimate in performance—a level of performance that can only be accommodated by parallelism. In fact, it is fair to say that all supercomputers are parallel computers. The converse is not true because there are other motivations (such as cost/performance and fault tolerance) for using parallelism.

This document provides an overview of the parallel computing techniques, vocabulary, currently available hardware architectures, and programming languages relevant to current supercomputers and parallel computers. With today's supercomputers and parallel computers providing an unprecedented amount of available computational power, an understanding of the critical concepts associated with these machines will provide a basis for appreciating their capabilities while also recognizing the present-day limitations of parallel processing.

What is a supercomputer? There is no fixed definition because the state of the art advances so rapidly that the most advanced computers soon become mediocre. In addition, there is no agreement among computer scientists on the definition of a supercomputer [Bell:89, NAS:89]. Historically, computer manufacturers have produced machines that challenged the state of the art and provided extraordinary performance and termed them supercomputers. There was prestige at stake in this activity, and though supercomputers were few in number, the problems they addressed were of national significance.

Traditionally, supercomputer-type problems involved computationally intensive problems in the subject areas of computational fluid dynamics, climatic modeling, molecular biology, chemical structures modeling, and electrical and mechanical design. These problems tended to be large, numerical problems—*number crunching* problems—and the computers to deal with them tended to emphasize outstanding performance on high-precision floating point arithmetic. By the 1970s it was feasible to establish a company completely dedicated to the production of this kind of computer, and Cray Research, Inc. was born. The delivery of the first Cray-1 in 1976 ushered in the modern era of supercomputing.

Today there are large problems that are not numerical in nature which require computer performance that challenges the state of the art. New modes of computing are required and new architectures are arising to fill the need. We review these in the following sections.

For the purposes of this document, the term *supercomputer* will be defined loosely to mean high-performance, general-purpose computers that exist today and can compete in average performance with the latest Cray and NEC computers. This report will discuss supercomputers as well as parallel machines that, in fact, are not traditionally considered to be supercomputers. A good example is the mini-supercomputers such as those made by Alliant.

Computer scientists tend to classify machines in different ways to provide different insight into the machine's architecture. One well-known approach developed by Michael Flynn classifies a machine by the type of instruction stream (a sequence of instructions performed by a computer) and data stream (a sequence of data that the computer performs instructions upon). Following Flynn's format, this report discusses machines that are designated as either *single instruction stream, multiple data stream* (SIMD) or *multiple instruction stream, multiple data stream* (MIMD) machines.

A second approach commonly used by researchers to classify machines is by the memory architecture of the machine. For example, *shared-memory* implies multiple processors sharing one common memory, whereas *distributed memory* implies memory localized to each processor. These terms will also be used extensively throughout this document. Although a high-performance computer may only have one processor, the emphasis of this report is on those computers that utilize multiple processors which run concurrently, thus the term *parallel computing*.

Needless to say, parallelism (doing more than one thing at the same time) has always been a major component of supercomputing. After all, once one has selected the fastest components available, some form of parallelism is the only way to make things go even faster. Supercomputers, even those that only have one processor, utilize parallelism at many levels of the architecture as its vehicle to increase speed. There are two basic techniques for achieving parallelism—*replication of function* and *pipelining*.

The analogy of a car wash illustrates these basic techniques. Washing a car consists of three steps: soaping, rinsing, and waxing (figure 1-1). If we consider the standard model of car washing, parallel operations are not practical, since some operations must be synchronized (a car must be soaped before it can be rinsed, and rinsed before it can be waxed). If we have three machines (replication of function) capable of washing cars and if we assume that each step takes one minute, then we can wash three cars in three minutes. But what if we only have one machine?

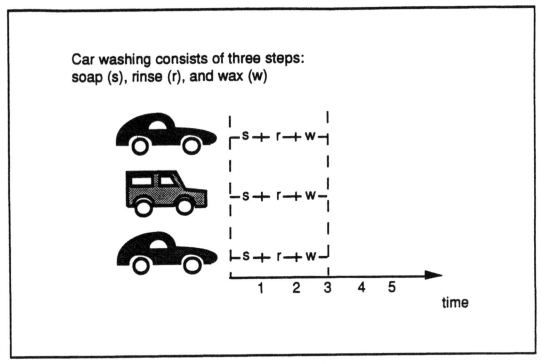

Figure 1-1. The Parallel Car Wash

If we completely soap, rinse, and wax each car one after the other, it takes nine minutes. We can do better, however, if we line up the cars one after the other. We still must wait three minutes to get the first car out, but we must wait only five minutes to get all three completely washed. This is called pipelining (figure 1-2). Variations of this technique have been used in supercomputers from the very beginning.

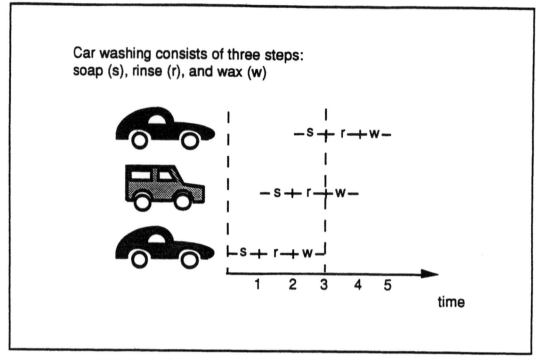

Figure 1-2. The Pipelined Car Wash

The value of replication of function is easy to understand. If a machine has two adders instead of one, it is then theoretically possible to perform two additions at once. Equally, if the machine possesses separate functional units to perform add and multiply instructions (as opposed to a single arithmetic/logic unit to do both), the potential exists for doing an add and a multiply at the same time.

Pipelining, on the other hand, provides a means for using available functionality more efficiently. For example, a floating point add (figure 1-3) involves four steps: compare exponents, shift the smaller augend until the exponents are equal, add the mantissas, and normalize the result.

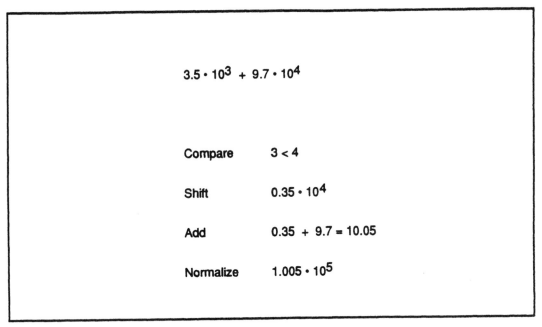

Figure 1-3. Floating Point Addition

A pipelined implementation of this operation works as follows: If we are adding 32 pairs of numbers, the machine starts by comparing the exponents of the first pair. Then, once the hardware that compares exponents has finished with the first pair, it can start work on the second, while the first pair enters the shifting stage, and so on.

Depending on the number of stages involved, pipelining can yield as much as an order of magnitude increase in speed over ordinary sequential processing. The principal difficulty is in keeping the pipeline full so that the processing hardware can be kept continuously busy. Much of the ingenuity in supercomputer design has been devoted to this problem.

A pipelined machine for matrix multiplication can be built using simple processors connected in a planar array (figure 1-4). Suppose we wish to multiply the 4-by-4 matrix **A** by the 4-by-4 matrix **B** to obtain the 4-by-4 matrix **C**. The element in the i-th row and j-th column of the **C** matrix is given by

cij = ai1*b1j + ai2*b2j + ai3*b3j + ai4*b4j.

At every clock cycle, elements of the **A** and **B** matrices are pumped into the horizontal and vertical pipelines, respectively. Results are accumulated at each processor so that when the input data has flowed through, the results are contained in the processors. Done this way, matrix multiplication can be performed in $O(n)$ operations [Jamieson:87]. An architecture like this is usually called a *systolic array*. Processors are connected to nearest neighbors, and the topology, in conjunction with synchronous clocking, causes each piece of data to arrive at the right processing element at the right time.

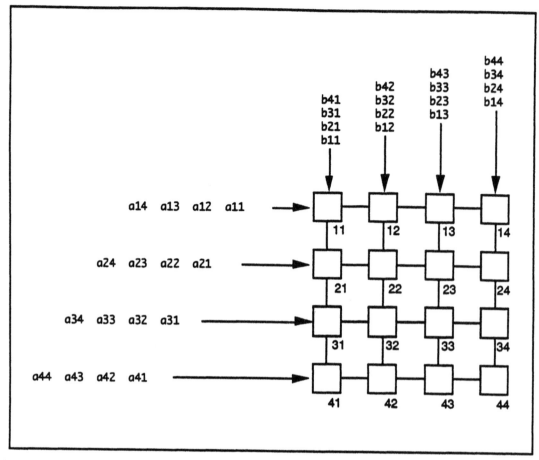

Figure 1-4. Systolic Processing

Systolic arrays are not sufficiently flexible for use as arithmetic processors in general purpose computers. However, the regular nature of most numerical problems provides a relatively simple approach to providing pipelines which can be kept full. A set of *vector operations* is defined to manipulate entire arrays. Because the same operation is performed on successive pairs of array elements (as in our example above), the pipeline is kept full. Since there is some overhead involved in starting up the vector computation, achieving adequate speed requires vectors of a certain minimum size to amortize the start-up time over a sufficient number of computations. This minimum size depends on the machine architecture and varies from machine to machine. Also, a vector register is designed to hold a maximum number of data elements. On the Alliant FX/Series machines the maximum number is 32; Cray machines allow 64, while some Japanese machines permit much larger vector (array) sizes by dynamic reconfiguration of vector register storage. Performance is best for arrays at the maximum size, but otherwise depends on the machine architecture. On the Alliant FX/Series machines, processing the maximum 32 elements with a vector instruction is approximately two to four times faster than processing the same elements with sequential scalar instructions [Alliant:88b].

It is possible, however, to do better than single pipelining. By using replication of function in concert with pipelining, an even higher degree of parallelism—hence, performance improvement—can be achieved.

In addition to the methods described above, most computing techniques must deal with the impossibility of constructing a memory that is both large enough to accommodate the size requirements of computationally intensive problems and fast enough to keep up with the fastest processing technology. Therefore, a hierarchy of memory (from large and slow to small and fast) is provided, and the problem of scheduling the movement of data among the different levels of the hierarchy becomes a critical issue for the architecture.

So far, we have examined only what we might call *fine-grained* parallelism—either how to do pieces of instructions in parallel or how to perform more than one individual instruction at the same time. At the most primitive level, the mechanics of a parallel computation are transparent to the programmer—the results appear as if performed in an entirely sequential fashion. However, as architectural devices such as vector instructions are included, either the programmer must account for them or sophisticated compilers will have to do so on the programmer's behalf. For regular problems such as traditional supercomputing problems, significant progress has been made toward automatic vectorization of code. Other kinds of code, however, still require the programmer's personal attention.

As the granularity of the parallelism increases, the problem of programming the architecture becomes more complicated. At the next level of granularity, called *medium-grained* parallelism, complete processing units are replicated. As before, breaking up pieces of numerical code to run on the various processors is the first step attempted in the parallelization process and a number of manufacturers are currently offering compilers that automatically accomplish this for their systems. FORTRAN and C are the most popular languages with automatic vectorization and parallelization capabilities.

However, for many problems, arranging *coarse-grained* parallelism is the programmer's task. The programmer must rely on programming languages (or language extensions) in which parallelism can be directly expressed. The most important of these, at least from the point of view of applications for the Department of Defense, is the Ada *tasking* model. Ada tasks can be executed in parallel with a rendezvous mechanism for specifying the required synchronization. It should be noted that there is software overhead involved in the implementation of Ada tasking and other such models. It is, accordingly, not always prudent to expect the same degree of performance improvement for programs that use such models as that achieved in programs that make extensive use of straightforward FORTRAN loops.

Finally, a few caveats. A classification of architectures is presented in the following sections. It is important not to take this classification scheme too seriously—the boundaries are always fuzzy and few machines are pure representations of a single type. Many are, in fact, obvious hybrids of the presented categories. Also, it is important to note that the value of any architecture is not absolute, but is strongly related to the type of problem one wishes to run. Machines that rely for their performance on catering to the regularity of numerical applications characteristically do not perform as well on symbolic computation. Thus, it is important not to measure the performance of a machine in terms of how quickly it might perform some ideal computation. Instead, it must be evaluated by careful analysis of how the specific intended application will run.

As the number of components in a system increases, so does the potential for malfunction. Providing continuity of operation and service in the presence of faults or malfunction is *fault-tolerant* computing. Since high-performance computers have always contained more components than ordinary computers, architectural attention to detection of and recovery from errors has always been important. Thus, the IBM 7030 (an early supercomputer) introduced error-correcting codes for memory when standard commercial practice had not even advanced as far as using parity. In fact, one third of the transistor count in the 7030 was devoted to error detection and correction. Nevertheless, little is said about fault tolerance in this document.

The fact of the matter is that for fine-grained parallelism, standard techniques are used for reliability. In contrast, providing system-level fault tolerance for coarse-grained parallelism remains to a large degree a research topic [Nelson:90]. While there are, in fact, commercial fault-tolerant multiprocessor computers available, these computers are primarily focused on the applications of very large databases and on-line transaction processing [Siewiorek:90].

Many of the parallel computers discussed in this document base their operating systems on UNIX. The security holes found in of UNIX are well known and documented [Garfinkel:91]. Therefore, this document does not address the computer security issue in regard to parallel computers. Finally, special-purpose computers, such as high-performance database machines and signal processors, are not discussed. (Some of the work in parallel signal processing that has been done at MITRE is described in [Cenkl:91, Nowacki:92].)

In the next section, we describe the various kinds of machine architectures. Section 3 then discusses software languages for parallel computers. Section 4 discusses the performance issues that should be considered when comparing one machine to another. Finally, section 5 is a short summary and provides a look into the future.

Appendix A provides descriptions of some current commercial offerings, illustrating the architectural alternatives discussed in this document. Appendix B provides a glossary of terms and abbreviations.

SECTION 2

MACHINE ARCHITECTURES

2.1 Introduction

There are several architectural dimensions to consider in parallel computing systems. How many processors are being used—tens, hundreds, or thousands? How are they interconnected? Can the system be expanded incrementally? Can the architecture be scaled up to support a large number of processors? How powerful are the individual processors? Are they single-bit processors, commercial microprocessors, or powerful custom processors? What is the granularity of parallelism that is supported: fine-grained (at the instruction level); medium-grained (at the cooperating concurrent task level with process synchronization occurring every few hundred machine instructions); or coarse-grained (at the nearly independent process level with process synchronization occurring every few thousand machine instructions)? This section addresses these considerations by discussing some commercially available machines.

2.2 Multiple Instruction Stream, Multiple Data Stream Machines

Multiple instruction stream, multiple data stream (MIMD) machines possess a number of processors that function asynchronously and independently; at any given time different processors may be executing different instructions on different pieces of data. They are ideal for medium to coarse-grained parallelism. The processors used in these machines range from conventional microprocessors, such as the Motorola 68040 used in the Myrias SPS-3 to powerful proprietary vector processors such as those used in the Cray Y-MP. This type of architecture has been used in a number of application areas; for example, computer-aided design/computer-aided manufacturing (CAD/CAM), simulation, modeling, and as communication switches. These MIMD machines can be broken down into the shared-memory and distributed-memory subcategories based on how their processors access memory.

Shared Memory. MIMD machines in this category have processors which share a common, central memory, as shown in figure 2-1, where the symbol **P** represents a processor. In its simplest form this entails attaching all the processors to a bus that connects them to memory. We shall call these *bus-based* shared-memory machines. Other machines which attempt to avoid some of the difficulties of the bus-based architecture will be discussed later as *extended* shared-memory and *hierarchical* shared-memory machines.

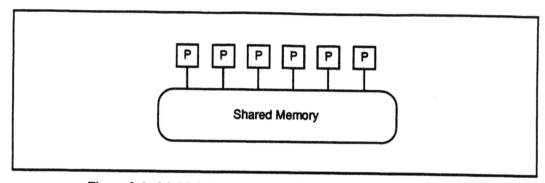

Figure 2-1. Multiple Instruction, Multiple Data, Shared Memory

Bus-Based. In addition to sharing information through central memory, these machines may have another bus that enables them to communicate directly with one another. This additional bus is used for controlling concurrency among the processors. Currently available shared-memory architectures that use a bus to connect processors to main memory are limited to supporting only a relatively small number of processors. For example, the Alliant computer supports a maximum of 28 processors, the Sequent computer a maximum of 30. This limitation is due to contention among processors for shared memory. The speed and bandwidth of the memory bus is a critical factor in such architectures. Thus, these machines can be incrementally expanded up to a point which is limited by the contention on the bus. Processors in these systems often have memory caches (discussed in section 4 on Performance Considerations) to minimize accesses to the shared main memory.

Extended. These architectures attempt to avoid or diminish the contention among processors for shared memory by subdividing the memory into a number of independent memory units and connecting them to the processors by an interconnection network. Many different interconnection schemes have been considered, and, indeed, many of these are quite similar to the distributed-memory architectures we will discuss later. However, they all provide hardware and software support for treating the memory units as a unified central memory. We shall discuss several of these schemes starting with the use of crossbar switches as an interconnection mechanism as illustrated in figure 2-2. Memory is divided into separate units; processors and memories are connected together in a two-dimensional array of wires linked by switches at each crossing point. Each processor is placed on a row, each memory unit on a column. A processor gains access to a memory unit by setting a switch at the intersection of the appropriate wires. A crossbar linking N processors to M memory units requires N times M switches. The cost of a 32-by-32 unit system containing 1,024 switches was considered prohibitive for commercial systems [Uhr:87] in the mid-eighties. Today Cogent uses four 32-by-32 crossbars to connect 32 processors, which allows as many as four processors to be connected to the same processor at the same time. Crossbar switching networks are still too expensive to be practical for connecting large numbers of processors. However, they may become more economical as optical interconnection becomes feasible [Sawchuk:87].

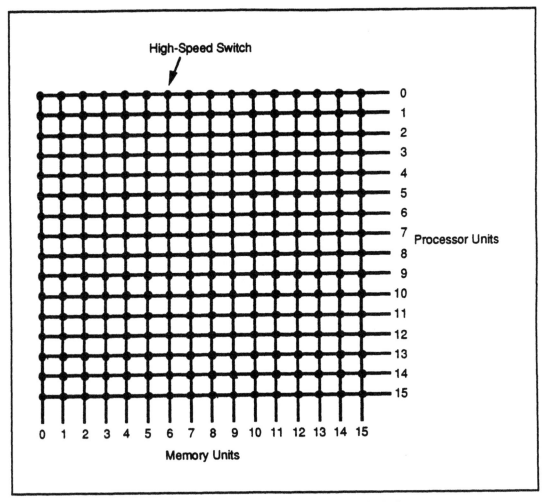

Figure 2-2. Crossbar Switch With 256 Switches

The BBN TC2000 is an example of a shared-memory architecture that uses a switching network to give processors access to memory units. In the TC2000, each processor is connected directly to a memory unit. When one processor needs access to the memory unit of another processor, it activates a switch. Rather than using a crossbar switch, the TC2000 uses BBN's third-generation Butterfly switch technology. The TC2000 Butterfly switch uses two stages of 8-input, 8-output Butterfly switch modules (SM) to interconnect up to 63 memory-processor modules as shown in figure 2-3. In general, connecting N processors using switches with M inputs and M outputs requires log MN banks of N/M switches. Thus, a three-stage Butterfly switch can support 512 modules.

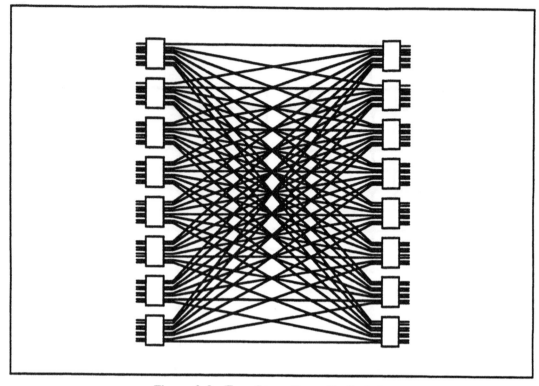

Figure 2-3. Two-Stage Butterfly Switch

Hierarchical. The Myrias SPS-3 is an example of a shared-memory architecture that uses a hierarchy of buses to give processors access to each other's memory (figure 2-4). In the Myrias, the four processors on a board communicate through an internodal bus. Sixteen boards may be placed in the same cage; two buses are used to support interboard communication. The two interboard buses connect to a crossbar switch that has five communication ports. These communication ports can be used to connect cages. In this way, the Myrias can be configured to support over a thousand processors.

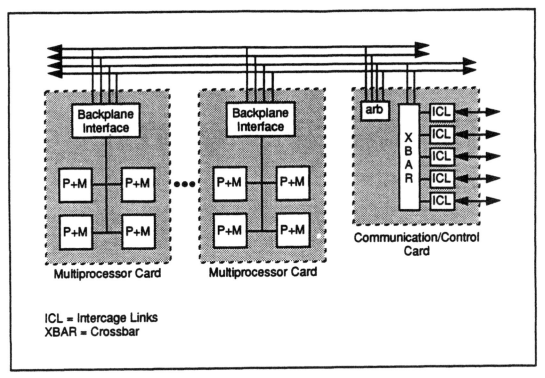

Figure 2-4. Myrias SPS-3

Distributed Memory. In this category, each processor has its own individual memory store—it does not share memory with other processors as shown in figure 2-5 where the symbols **P** and **M** represent a processor and memory. For data to be shared, it must be passed from one processor to another in the form of messages. Since the processors do not share memory, contention among processors is not as great a problem. Thus, these systems would seem to more readily scale up to support a large number of processors.

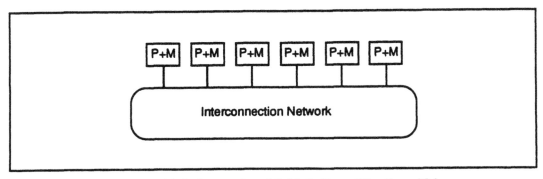

Figure 2-5. Multiple Instruction, Multiple Data, Distributed Memory

For a large number of processors, it is not economically feasible to connect every processor directly to every other processor. So the approach taken is to connect each processor to only a few others. The original systems designed in this fashion were inefficient, because messages were routed through intermediate processors on their way to a final destination processor. In such a system, the amount of time spent by processors performing simple message routing can be substantial. Also, the difference in the amount of time needed to send a message to a directly connected processor versus an indirectly connected processor may be substantial. This led to systems designed to reduce the number of hops between processors (systems such as hypercubes or reconfigurable networks) and research into algorithms designed to localize data transfer among processors. Providing special-purpose processors for message routing, often termed *wormhole routing*, can eliminate some of these difficulties [Dally:87]. Among the commercially available processors in this category, the interconnection schemes that seem to be the most popular are the hypercube and mesh.

Hypercube. In a hypercube system containing four processors (called a 2-cube), a processor and memory module are placed at each vertex of a square as illustrated in figure 2-6a where the symbols **P** and **M** represent a processor and memory. If processors on the diagonal vertices send messages to each other, those messages must be forwarded through one of the directly connected processors. By definition, the diameter of the system is the minimum number of steps it takes for one processor to send a message to the processor that is furthest away. The diameter of a 2-cube is therefore 2.

In a hypercube system containing eight processors (called a 3-cube), a processor and memory module are placed at each vertex of a cube. Each processor is directly connected to three others. The diameter of a 3-cube is 3. For example, in figure 2-6b, it takes three steps for processor 000 to send a message to processor 111 (i.e., 000 to 001 to 101 to 111).

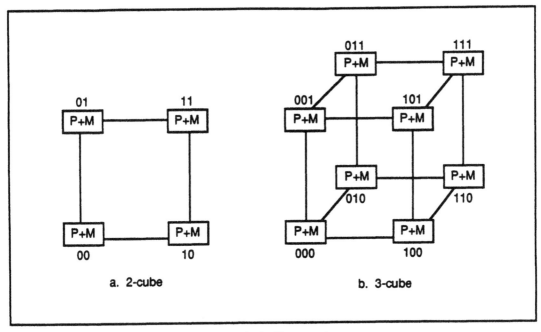

Figure 2-6. Hypercubes

In general, for a system that contains 2^N processors (called an N-cube), each processor is directly connected to N other processors, and the diameter of the system is N. One of the drawbacks of the commercially available systems that use the hypercube topology is that they must be configured in powers of two. For example, it is possible to have a system that contains 64 or 128 processors, but not one that contains 90 processors. Further, if the system is to be used by multiple users, each user must be assigned a subcube that contains a power of 2 processors. Even though a user needs only five processors for a particular application, eight must still be allocated.

The Intel iPSC/860 is a commercially available machine with a hypercube interconnection network. Its maximum configuration supports up to 128 processors. In the iPSC/860, each computational reduced instruction set computer (RISC) processor is connected to a message-routing processor; these routers are connected in a hypercube. When one computational processor needs to send a message to another computational RISC processor, it passes the message to its router, as illustrated in figure 2-7. The message is passed from router to router (along a specified path which contains the fewest nodes) until the router that is connected to the destination computational processor is reached, at which point the message is delivered to that computational processor.

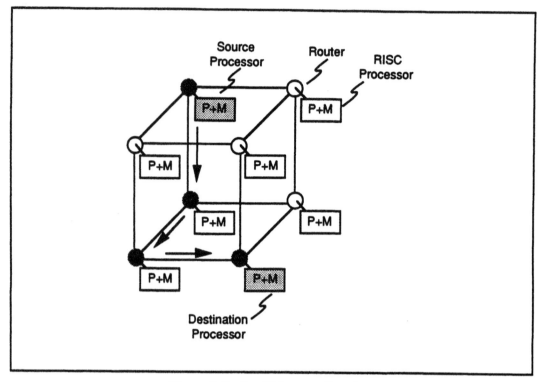

Figure 2-7. Intel Message Routing

The iPSC/860 uses a derivative of wormhole routing called *direct connect routing*. In this routing scheme, the path from the sending computational processor's router to the destination processor's router is established and held until the message has been completely transmitted. The advantage of this scheme is that once a message establishes a path or circuit, the message moves directly to the destination without further delay. A possible disadvantage of this scheme is that if a long message must be passed, the entire path is held until that message is completely transmitted. If other messages need to use any portion of the path, they must wait.

The NCUBE 2 processors also use a high-speed hardware message routing unit to reduce communication overhead. This unit replaces previous store-and-forward schemes for messages sent beyond nearest neighbor processors and thus performs many times faster. It allows direct pass-through of messages to other processors without interrupting intermediate processors or requiring message data to be stored in their memory, and messages can be of any length.

Mesh. In a mesh, processors are placed in a two-dimensional grid, as depicted in figure 2-8, where the symbols **P** and **M** represent a processor and memory. Each of the processors is connected to its four immediate neighbors. Wraparound connections are also sometimes provided at the edges to further reduce the communication diameter.

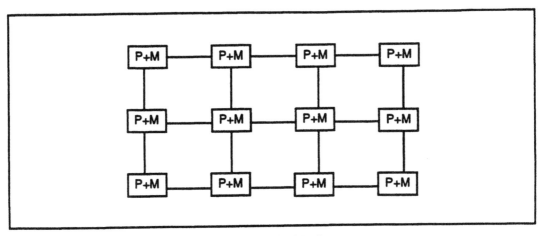

Figure 2-8. Mesh

Although the Symult S2010 (previously called the Ametek S2010) is no longer commercially available, its architecture provides an interesting contrast to the Intel iPSC/860. The Symult S2010 is a system that uses a mesh interconnection scheme to support up to 1,024 processors. In the S2010, each computational 68020 processor is connected to a message-routing processor, and then the message-routing processors are connected in a mesh. When one computational processor needs to send a message to another, it passes the message to its router processor as shown in figure 2-9. The message is passed from router to router the appropriate number of steps in the horizontal direction. Finally, the message is passed the appropriate number of steps in the vertical direction until the router that is connected to the destination is reached.

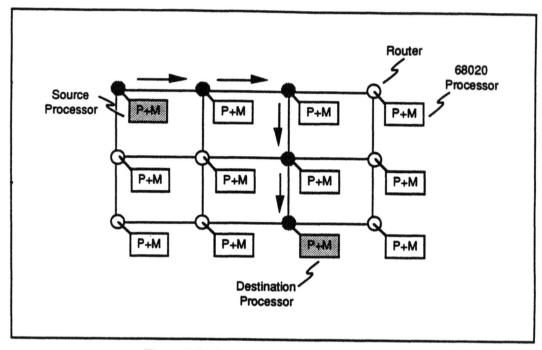

Figure 2-9. Symult S2010 Message Routing

The Symult S2010 does not use Intel's direct-connect routing technique. Rather, messages are *packetized* (that is, broken into pieces of fixed length); each router processor then uses fair arbitration to determine which packet to pass next. An advantage of this scheme over direct-connect routing is that other messages may not be delayed as long, when a long message is sent on a path that uses a portion of the path they require. On the other hand, packet management entails some amount of overhead that is avoided in direct-connect routing. This overhead results from organizing the message to be sent into packets at the source and reorganizing back into the original message format at the destination.

An advantage of the mesh over the hypercube topology is that mesh systems need not be configured in powers of two. A disadvantage is that the diameter of the mesh network is greater than the hypercube for systems with more than four processors. For example, in a 64-processor hypercube, the diameter is six, while in a 64-processor mesh with no wraparound connections, the diameter is 14.

According to results obtained from the California Institute of Technology, the use of special-purpose processors for routing messages should reduce message-passing time sufficiently to allow a two-dimensional mesh to support as many as four thousand processors [Dally:87]. For more than that number, a three-dimensional mesh is suggested.

Reconfigurable. In a reconfigurable system, programmable switches allow users to select a logical processor interconnection topology that best matches their application's communication patterns. In some cases, the processor topology can be defined by the user at run time. The Meiko Computing Surface is an example of a system whose connectivity can be manually or electronically reconfigured into various topologies such as rings, grids, low-order hypercubes, and pipelines.

2.3 Single Instruction Stream, Multiple Data Stream Machines

In single instruction stream, multiple data stream (SIMD) machines, all processors execute the same instruction, at the same time, on different data, under the control of a central control unit as shown in figure 2-10 where symbols **P** and **M** represent processor and memory. These systems can be massively parallel, generally possessing a very large number of simple (in some cases only 1-bit) processors. For this approach, speed comes from having thousands of processors. For example, the Connection Machine Model CM-2 has 64,000 1-bit processors. This type of architecture has proven successful in a number of application areas; for example, image processing, partial differential equations by relaxation methods, matrix operations, fast Fourier transforms, and database searches, all of which exhibit fine-grained parallelism.

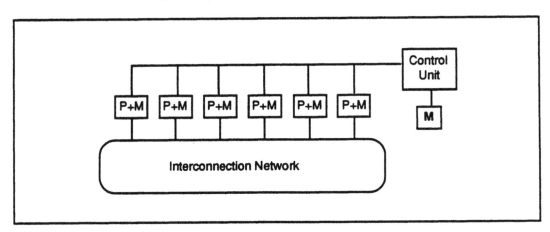

Figure 2-10. Single Instruction, Multiple Data, Distributed Memory

To pass data from one processor to another, SIMD processors may be interconnected in different ways. In the CM-2 and the Active Memory Technology DAP 610, processors are connected in a two-dimensional mesh. In addition, in the CM-2, each processor is connected to a router processor, and router processors are connected in a hypercube. In the DAP, on the other hand, there is an orthogonal bus system that connects all the processing elements in each row and all the processing elements in each column. Structuring these row and column data paths in this manner provides a capability to simultaneously broadcast messages to all processors in a given row or column.

Image processing is an application that is suitable for SIMD architectures. Many of the computations involve the same operations performed on similar data elements simultaneously. Let us assume our image is given by a two-dimensional array of integers between 0 and 16 representing gray scale values (figure 2-11). Important goals of an image recognition system are the elimination of noise and the detection of edges.

0	0	0	0	0	0	0	0	0	0	0	0	0	0	0	3
0	0	0	0	0	0	0	0	0	0	0	0	0	0	0	0
0	0	4	10	10	0	10	0	0	0	0	10	10	10	0	0
0	0	6	10	10	10	10	8	0	0	0	10	10	10	0	0
0	0	8	10	10	10	10	10	0	0	0	10	10	10	0	0
0	0	12	10	10	10	10	10	0	0	0	10	10	10	0	0
0	0	10	10	12	10	11	10	0	0	0	10	10	10	0	0
0	0	10	11	15	10	12	10	6	0	0	0	0	0	2	0
0	0	4	10	10	10	10	3	0	0	0	0	0	0	0	0
0	0	3	10	10	10	10	5	0	0	0	0	0	0	0	0
0	0	4	10	10	10	10	2	0	0	0	0	0	0	0	0
0	0	4	10	10	10	7	3	0	0	0	0	5	0	0	0
0	0	0	0	6	8	0	0	0	0	0	0	0	0	0	0
0	0	0	0	0	0	0	0	0	0	0	0	0	0	0	0
0	0	0	0	0	0	0	0	0	0	0	0	0	0	5	0
0	0	0	0	0	0	0	0	0	0	0	0	0	0	0	0

Figure 2-11. Original Array

Let's examine how a simple algorithm might work on a SIMD. Suppose we assign each element of the array to a processor. In order to identify the edge of an object in a picture, we need to identify the places where the light intensity changes sharply. To obtain an estimate of the direction of maximum change (squared gradient) of the light intensity at a point, we can use the formula:

$$\left(\frac{\partial I}{\partial x}\right)^2 + \left(\frac{\partial I}{\partial y}\right)^2 \approx (E - W)^2 + (N - S)^2$$

In this formula, E, W, N, and S represent the values of the array elements to the east, west, north, and south of a point, that is, the value contained in the memory of the processor to the east, west, north, and south of the array element that represents the point. The symbol I represents light intensity at a point.

If we perform the necessary computations all over the image, we obtain a new array, which we call the squared gradient array (figure 2-12). In the squared gradient array, there are high values at places where brightness changes rapidly, that is, at the edges of the objects. While in regions of constant brightness, the value is zero. Where there is noise, the output is non-zero but relatively small.

```
  0    0    0    0    0    0    0    0    0    0    0    0    0    0    0    0
  9    0   16  100  100    0  100    0    0    0    0  100  100  100    0    0
  0   16  136  136  200  100  100  164    0    0  100  200  100  200  100    0
  0   36  116   16    0  100    4  200   64    0  100  100    0  100  100    0
  0   64  136    4    0    0    0  104  100    0  100  100    0  100  100    0
  0  144  104    4    4    0    1  100  100    0  100  100    0  100  100    0
  0  100  104    5   25    1    4  121  136    0  100  200  100  200  104    0
  0  100  157   25    5    9    1   85  100   36    0  100  100  104    0    0
  0   16  149   37   25    0   53  125   45    0    0    0    0    0    4    0
  0    9  100   49    0    0   25  101   25    0    0    0    0    0    0    0
  0   16  101   36    0    0   73  104    4    0    0    0   25    0    0    0
  0   16  116  136   16   13  149   53    9    0    0   25    0   25    0    0
  0    0   16  136  164  136  113    9    0    0    0    0   25    0    0    0
  0    0    0    0   36   64    0    0    0    0    0    0    0    0   25    0
  0    0    0    0    0    0    0    0    0    0    0    0    0   25    0    0
  0    0    0    0    0    0    0    0    0    0    0    0    0    0    0    0
```

Figure 2-12. Squared Gradient Array

If we threshold at 50, the noise is removed. Thus, we obtain the final array, with the edges of objects clearly marked and the noise removed (figure 2-13).

0	0	0	0	0	0	0	0	0	0	0	0	0	0	0	0
0	0	0	100	100	0	100	0	0	0	0	100	100	100	0	0
0	0	136	136	200	100	100	164	0	0	100	200	100	200	100	0
0	0	116	0	0	100	0	200	64	0	100	100	0	100	100	0
0	64	136	0	0	0	0	104	100	0	100	100	0	100	100	0
0	144	104	0	0	0	0	100	100	0	100	100	0	100	100	0
0	100	104	0	0	0	0	121	136	0	100	200	100	200	104	0
0	100	157	0	0	0	0	85	100	0	0	100	100	104	0	0
0	0	149	0	0	0	53	125	0	0	0	0	0	0	0	0
0	0	100	0	0	0	0	101	0	0	0	0	0	0	0	0
0	0	101	0	0	0	73	104	0	0	0	0	0	0	0	0
0	0	116	136	0	0	149	53	0	0	0	0	0	0	0	0
0	0	0	136	164	136	113	0	0	0	0	0	0	0	0	0
0	0	0	0	0	64	0	0	0	0	0	0	0	0	0	0
0	0	0	0	0	0	0	0	0	0	0	0	0	0	0	0
0	0	0	0	0	0	0	0	0	0	0	0	0	0	0	0

Figure 2-13. Final Array

The computations involved in this three step algorithm used values of neighboring image cells or the value of the cell itself. In each of the three steps, the required values can be obtained and the computations performed synchronously. This is an ideal application for a SIMD architecture. It is not surprising that NASA has used SIMD's for image processing applications

2.4 Networks of Machines

Computer networks can be used to interconnect independent machines. Networks are a mechanism to increase computational power. First, networks allow users to utilize more than one high-performance computer to carry out a computation at a coarse-grain level. Secondly, networks, by virtue of their interconnection of different machine types, allow sharing of limited computational resources.

In fact, most commercial manufacturers today provide both hardware and software interfaces for integrating their machines into at least local area network environments.

One research effort is the CEDAR project at the University of Illinois in which clusters of modified Alliant FX/8s are networked together.

Local area networks can be used to couple many machines. If appropriate software is added, as with MITRE's own Network Batching System, these networks can be used as loosely coupled MIMD computers. MITRE has been able to make N Sun-3 computers yield an N-fold speed improvement over one computer in executing the quadratic sieve integer factoring algorithm [Silverman:88, 89, 90,91]. The result is at least a 33:1 price/performance improvement over what a Cray X-MP can achieve. The chief reason for this is that the algorithm is designed so that it requires little processor-to-processor communication. Such algorithms are as yet rather rare, but research effort is being focused on their development. One can often trade communications for additional computation, yet still speed up actual algorithm execution time.

2.5 Parallelism Within Processors

So far we have been considering architectures that realize parallelism by incorporating many processors which can be utilized simultaneously for problem solving. Indeed, this kind of parallelism is emphasized in this document. In this subsection, however, we will concentrate on architectural features which promote parallelism within a single processor. Since these features are developed most fully in modern conventional supercomputers (such as the Cray, NEC, CONVEX, Fujitsu, and Hitachi supercomputers), we will use this class of machine as a point of departure in the following discussion.

In previous subsections, the basic mechanism for parallelism has been *replication* where many processors are used. *Pipelining* (as described in the introduction, section 1) becomes the basic mechanism for providing parallelism within processors, although replication (especially in the utilization of many pipelines) is also important. Furthermore, we should observe that most modern supercomputers contain more than one processor, so that above the processor level they exhibit the architecture of a shared memory MIMD as described in subsection 2.2.

Every supercomputer designer has a number of bottlenecks to eliminate which may yield to parallelism as a solution. To begin with, many arithmetic instructions take several clock periods to execute. (For example, a floating-point addition on the Cray X-MP processor takes six clock periods.) Clearly much can be gained by parallelism. For example, if we replicated the adders and used them alternately, we could do twice as many adds at the same time. Indeed, this approach was taken in earlier computers including the CDC 6600 designed by Seymour Cray. In modern supercomputers, however, pipelining is typically implemented first, because it does not introduce the communications and synchronization penalties frequently associated with replication. Consequently, supercomputer instruction processors (usually called functional units because they perform specific functions) are routinely pipelined and can, therefore, accept a new instruction every clock period. Usually there are many different functional units to perform the many different kinds of instructions (on the X-MP processor there is a total of 13 or 14) so there is replication parallelism as well.

To make all of this work, the pipelines must be kept full of instructions and data. To make sure that instructions are always available, high speed buffers are placed between the main memory and the functional units. (On the X-MP these buffers can hold 512 16-bit instructions.) So that data can be prefetched well in advance of use, many sets of registers are available to act as data buffers.

Complicated schemes for accessing the main memory are generally another hallmark of conventional supercomputers. Although fast memories are used in these machines, they are still substantially slower than the CPU clock rate. For example, on the X-MP memory access time is four clock periods. Complex interleaving schemes are employed to provide a continuous flow from memory to the CPUs at the CPU clock rate in order to keep the pipelines full. Figure 2-14 shows the memory access scheme of a two CPU Cray X-MP. Each CPU has four ports to the memory which are connected via a cross bar switch to four lines each of which goes to one of the four memory sections. Each section in turn consists of eight one megabyte memory banks. Addresses are alternated among the sections and banks to minimize the probability of memory conflict. Interestingly, when either CPU has to initiate an instruction fetch sequence, all eight ports are used simultaneously for that purpose.

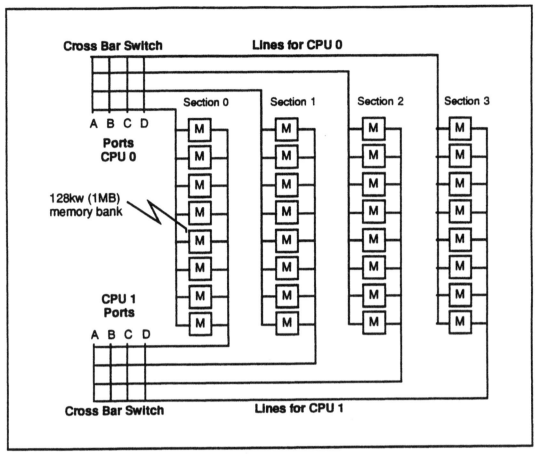

Figure 2-14. Cray X-MP Memory Connections for 2 CPUs

Even using the sophisticated scheme depicted in figure 2-14, keeping the various pipelines full is difficult so that the hardware's maximum computing capabilities can rarely be exploited. For this reason, supercomputer designers added *vector instructions*, described in section 1, to improve performance. These instructions operate on entire arrays of data. With vector instructions, once the pipeline fills it will remain full until the processing is complete. An example of this is illustrated in figure 2-15 depicting a snapshot of a vector operation taken in the middle of its computational sequence. A 64 element vector X is stored in vector register V0 and a 64 element vector Y is stored in vector register V1. The X-MP is executing the vector add instruction which will cause the 64 element vector Z = X + Y to be computed and stored in vector register V7. As can be seen from the figure, parts of eight different adds are going on at the same time.

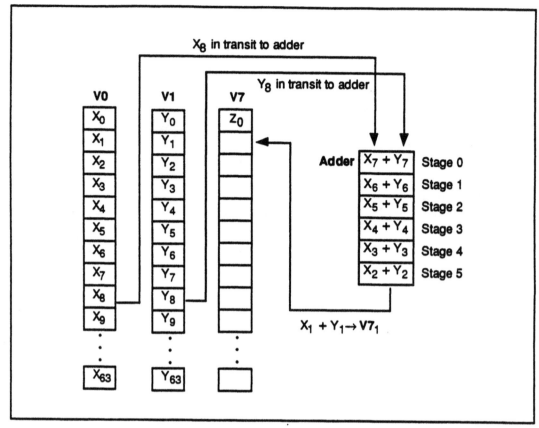

Figure 2-15. Snapshot of Cray X-MP Vector Operation

The essence of SIMD parallelism is that the same operation is being performed on different data elements at the same time. When the programmer uses a vector operation, he is telling the system that it may perform the same operation on different data elements at the same time. Thus, from the programmer's perspective a vector operation is a SIMD operation. In subsection 2.3 describing SIMD computers, we described how SIMD parallelism can be provided by replication. In a vector processor, it is typically provided by pipelining. Therefore, a vector processor is essentially a *pipelined SIMD* and is sometimes referred to as such in the literature [Hockney: 88].

The essence of MIMD parallelism is that different operations are being performed on different data elements at the same time. It is also possible to implement a MIMD by pipelining within a single processor. The process execution module (PEM) of the Denelcor Heterogeneous Element Processor (HEP) is a good example of MIMD pipelining. The HEP is no longer being manufactured, but is interesting enough to warrant further discussion. This machine could have up to 16 PEMs connected by a packet switched network and up to 128 data memory modules (DMM). Thus, the HEP is a shared memory MIMD where each processor in turn is a *pipelined MIMD*.

However, the control structure of a PEM itself, presented in simplified form in figure 2-16, is the interesting feature of the HEP. Each circle in the diagram represents the control tag of one of up to fifty simultaneous processes. These processes share an eight-stage instruction-execution pipeline. When the tag of a process enters the first stage, the corresponding instruction is fetched from the one megaword local instruction store. (Since the instructions are stored locally, the characterization of this architecture as a shared memory MIMD is slightly inaccurate.) When it enters the second stage, the corresponding data are fetched if they reside in the local register or constant stores. If a main memory reference is required, however, the control tag is "waved off" and sent to the SFU queue (SFU stands for shared-memory functional unit). The tag of the process will then be reentered into the instruction execution pipeline when the memory operand is available.

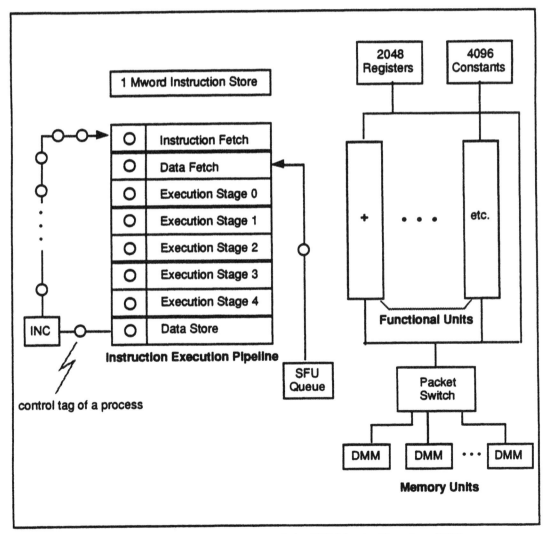

Figure 2-16. Control Structure of the PEM in the Denelcor HEP

The next four stages correspond to the stages of the functional units which are pipelined as is customary in supercomputers. When the last stage is entered, the result of the operation will be stored. Finally, after leaving the pipeline the instruction counter in the control tag will be incremented (as represented by the box labeled "INC" in the diagram), so that it will be ready to reenter the pipeline at a later time. In some sense, the PEM works in much the same way as a "time-sliced" multiprogramming system but with a time slice of one clock period!

"Waving off" the control tag whose memory operand is not yet available is perhaps the most interesting of the ideas presented above. The notion that the execution of instructions can be ordered by the availability of data is carried further in data flow machines where it becomes the principal control mechanism. To date, however, only experimental, general-purpose, data flow machines have been constructed although several coarse-grained data flow architectures for signal processing are currently marketed. A related topic is the concept of data flow languages, discussed in section 3.5, which are in some sense the natural languages for these machines.

In recent years a new category of architectures has evolved to achieve parallelism within a processor. While the vector machines have been very successful, not all code can be readily vectorized. Therefore, there has been some impetus to find architectures that can execute more than one instruction per clock cycle without resorting to vector operations. Such architectures are called *superscalar*. They borrow from the successful vector machines the idea of multiple pipelined arithmetic units, so that several operations can be going on at the same time. Additionally, the architectures usually employ a RISC CPU so that most instructions only require one or two clock periods for execution; thus, the number and length of pipelines required to obtain speedup may be reduced.

Data fetch bottlenecks are ameliorated by extensive use of caches and by providing hardware support for performing instructions out of order thus allowing the data fetch instructions to be issued as early as possible. In the IBM POWER architecture, for example, there is a register renaming capability, so that if an instruction to fetch data into a register that is in use is encountered, the data can be fetched into an unused register which will be renamed to be the correct one at the appropriate time.

Caches are also used to avoid instruction fetch bottlenecks. Moreover, since the goal is to execute more than one instruction per clock period, there is a requirement for a facility to fetch and decode several instructions at the same time. This can be accomplished either by using a long instruction word which contains several instructions or by building into the instruction cache/buffer the capability of providing several instructions during a single clock period. The former approach has been popular in signal processing machines, and it did make a brief appearance in the Multiflow Trace architecture (where packing instructions into the long word was supported by innovative compiler technology) before Multiflow went out of business. This approach can currently be found in Intel's iWARP architecture, which may be considered to be on the boundary between the categories of general-purpose and special-purpose computers (signal processing). The second approach which involves fetching more than one instruction per clock period is more common in current superscale chips.

Thus, as we can see, increasingly ingenious strategies have been formulated to achieve greater parallelism and faster performance in individual processors. It is generally believed that the future of high-performance computing rests with the massively parallel approaches described in the previous subsections. The MIMDs described in subsection 2.2 will require increasingly capable processors—processors which will undoubtedly incorporate many of the ideas set forth in this subsection.

SECTION 3

LANGUAGES FOR PARALLEL COMPUTERS

3.1 Introduction

Today's parallel computers have extraordinary computational power. The question is whether this capability can be used effectively to increase application performance. The answer to this question depends on how well the hardware and the application software interface. Since the application software consists of an algorithm, the programming language, and the compiler, the processing power of the parallel computer is often realized only when this software explicitly exploits the hardware.

For multiple processors to work together, the various routines executed on these processors must communicate and synchronize with one another. Without communication and synchronization mechanisms, code may be executed using old values of data rather than the current values, and variables may be modified by more than one process, leading to unintended results. Communication also allows the execution of one process to influence the execution of another process.

Discussed in the following section will be the various synchronization mechanisms that are used to interface the software with the hardware and the methods currently used for parallelizing them. In sections 3.3 through 3.8, some of the latest approaches to parallel programming, including new languages and software paradigms currently being researched, are discussed.

3.2 Synchronization Operations and Methods

Synchronization is required when processes communicate with one another because of process dependencies. Typically, a process, P2, must wait until another process, P1, completes an action before it can begin its action. For example, let the shared variable $x = 0$ and let

$$P1: \quad x = x + 1 \qquad\qquad P2: \quad x = x + 2.$$

Although both of the statements associated with processes P1 and P2 look like *atomic* statements (an indivisible operation), in fact, they are not. Both statements actually take three steps to execute. First, the value of x has to be fetched from memory and stored in a register; second, the constant 1 or 2 is added to the register; and finally, the result in the register is stored back in x. When processes P1 and P2 are executed sequentially, x has the value 3. However, if processes P1 and P2 are executed concurrently with no synchronization, x may have a value of 1, 2, or 3 as a final result because the three steps of P1 and P2 may be intertwined. Therefore, synchronization is required to ensure the correct value of x by forcing sequential execution of P1 and P2. Synchronization that ensures that a sequence of statements is treated atomically is called *mutual exclusion*. A set of statements that must be executed atomically is called a *critical section*.

One way of providing synchronization is by using semaphores. A *semaphore* is a shared variable that indicates the number of processes attempting to enter their critical section. Typically, two atomic operations, P (different from processes P1 and P2) and V, are associated with semaphores. The operation P allows a process to acquire permission to enter its critical section, and the operation V records the termination of one process' critical section so that another process may enter its critical section. Protecting critical sections with semaphores is easy; all the hard work is done in P and V. The operation P is placed before the critical section and V afterwards. For example, let a semaphore, denoted as s, be a nonnegative integer initialized to one. Looking at the previous example, the processes P1 and P2, could be rewritten as [Whiddett:87]:

```
P1:    P(s)                    P2:    P(s)
       x = x + 1                      x = x + 2
       V(s)                           V(s)
```

When a process wants to enter its critical section, it executes P(s). P(s) performs several operations atomically. It reads and tests s. If s has a value greater than zero, it decrements s and allows the process to enter its critical section. If s is equal to zero, the process is not allowed to enter its critical section. V(s) also performs operations atomically. It reads and increments s' value. Suppose s is equal to one, when P1 executes P(s). P(s) decrements s and allows P1 to enter its critical section. Now suppose P2 wants to enter its critical section, it begins by executing P(s). However, this time s has a value of zero, so P2 may not begin executing its critical section. When P1 is finished executing its critical section, it executes V(s). V(s) increments s. Now suppose P2 executes P(s) again. This time s is greater than zero, so P decrements s and allows P2 to enter its critical section.

Now assuming processes P1 and P2 are intended to be executed serially, the correct answer, x=3, is ensured. The operations P and V can be implemented in hardware or in software using *spinlocks* or system calls to the kernel. Spinlocks are shared variables that, when set to a prespecified value by a process, signal that a condition has occurred. A process waits for that condition by repeatedly testing the shared variable. The repeated testing is also called *spinning*, thus, the name spinlock. The main disadvantage of using spinlocks to implement synchronization is that spinning wastes processor cycles that could otherwise be used for useful work. Using system calls to the kernel, on the other hand, is ideally suited for implementing synchronization without using a spinning mechanism. The kernel keeps track of which processes are ready to execute by maintaining a ready list. Processes that are blocked by a semaphore are not entered on the ready list and are not executed.

Using either spinlocks or semaphores for implementing synchronization in a parallel program can make the algorithm unstructured and prone to errors. Typical mistakes are, for example, invoking either P or V and not the other, or using P on one semaphore and the matching V on a different semaphore. These types of mistakes may cause *deadlock*. Deadlock occurs when two or more processes are waiting for events that will never occur.

Other synchronization techniques have been developed which avoid these types of errors. One of these is the concept *monitors*. A monitor is a construct which encapsulates both the resource definition and the operations that manipulate it [Andrews:83]. Inside a monitor, permanent variables are used to store the state of the resource. These can be accessed only from within the monitor and are reset between the various monitor operation calls. Control of the monitor occurs at the monitor boundary, and fairness is enforced by means of a wait queue. As an example, a monitor "x_mon" written to control the reading and writing of the shared variable x would take the following structure:

```
x_mon: monitor
    var x_being_written: boolean
    procedure read_x
        if (x_being_written) then
            wait
        else
            read x
    end read_x

    procedure read_x_done
        signal
    end read_x_done

    procedure write_x
        if (x_being_written) then
            wait
        else
            x_being_written = T
            write x
    and write_x

    procedure write_x_done
        x_being_written = F
        signal
    end write_x_done
end x_mon
```

The boolean variable x_being_written is used to control access to the operations within the monitor. In order for a process to read x, x_being_written must be false. This ensures that no process will access the variable at the same time another process is updating it. On the other hand, it also allows multiple reads to occur concurrently. In order to ensure fair scheduling of the waiting processes, the next process in the queue is signalled when the operations are completed.

Languages used to program parallel computers have to express the parallelism in an application or its algorithm to each parallel processor and provide mechanisms for communication and synchronization. Without appropriate programming languages and paradigms, the computational speed of parallel computers cannot be fully utilized and errors may be introduced into the application programs. Furthermore, designing and coding parallel programs is difficult and getting the programs to run is complicated, because many implementation and operational details have to be considered in addition to just coding and testing the algorithm. It is not a simple matter to write parallel programs that are syntactically and functionally correct, efficient, portable, and cost-effective. Therefore, identifying suitable languages for parallel computers becomes an important issue.

Although a programmer tries to think like a computer, this time-honored method is almost impossible to use with parallel processes because the sequence of events cannot always be predicted in advance. Moreover, when the code is executed, the code should be efficient. Achieving maximum code speedup on a parallel computer requires a deep understanding of the underlying parallel architecture. Astute decisions have to be made when sections of code are singled out for concurrent execution, and other decisions need to be made concerning how that concurrent execution should take place.

Currently, application programs that exploit the computational power of a supercomputer or a parallel computer tend to be tailored specifically to that hardware. As a consequence, the code is not easily portable to other hardware platforms. The price paid to gain an increased level of performance may be too high if the code takes too long to develop or is unmaintainable. The important choice of a parallel language or programming paradigm can greatly enhance or detract from the programmer's ability to write correct, efficient, portable, and cost-effective code.

3.3 Established Languages

For many, FORTRAN is currently the language of choice for parallel computers due to its maturity and the sophistication of its compilers. However, other languages, such as C, have a growing user base. Moreover, the operating systems of many parallel supercomputers are based on UNIX, and C is a very popular programming language with users of this operating system. Clearly the use of FORTRAN and C have important advantages because these languages have gained wide acceptance in commercial and scientific contexts. However, neither language was ever intended to operate on multiprocessor parallel architectures. Parallelizing compilers, annotations, language extensions, and library calls are four basic approaches that are used to overcome the inherent limitations of these conventional imperative languages.

Compilers. A parallel computer with a parallelizing compiler permits the programmer to write conventional sequential code without the need for identifying areas for potential concurrent or vector execution. The compiler identifies pieces of the program code that may be run concurrently or can be vectorized. Existing programs can be run on these parallel computers in this manner using familiar languages, and the programmer is freed from concerns about where the inherent parallelism exists in his code.

Current parallelizing compilers primarily look at loops to identify parallelism since this is where most of the execution time for numerical programs is spent. The compiler may generate code to *concurrentize* loops for execution on multiprocessor machines or *vectorize* loops for execution on machines that support vector processing. (Some compilers, like the Alliant's FX/FORTRAN compiler, will generate concurrent code for some loops and vector code for other loops.) If each iteration of a loop is independent of other iterations, synchronization between iterations is not needed, and the loops may execute concurrently to the extent that processors are available. On the other hand, if an iteration is dependent on any of the previous iterations, synchronization is required between iterations. The loops may then execute partially concurrent, that is, up to the synchronization point. Points in the code where synchronization is needed are identified by the compiler examining the data-dependence relations of code statements. Data-dependence testing is required for any form of automatic parallelism detection performed prior to run time.

Some parallelizing compilers also look for opportunities to vectorize; that is, to utilize vector processors. In fact, automatic recognition of parallel constructs by a commercial compiler is a recent innovation, while compilers that automatically identify opportunities for vectorization have been in existence for over ten years. It is not surprising that the techniques which automatically detect opportunities for vectorization were modified and enhanced to detect opportunities for concurrentization. The FX/FORTRAN compiler for the Alliant FX/80 is an excellent example of an optimizing compiler that looks for opportunities to create both concurrent and vectorized code.

Annotations. A parallelizing compiler, however, makes conservative decisions about where to concurrentize and vectorize and may miss opportunities for parallelization. If more information were made available to the compiler, further optimization could be performed resulting in the generation of more efficient code and the identification of other opportunities for parallelization. In the fairly typical FORTRAN code example,

```
      DO 5 I=1,N
  5      A(K(I)) = A(K(I)) + C(I)
```

most parallelizing compilers will generate sequential code because these compilers do not typically know if each element in K is unique. Annotations and language extensions are techniques that have been devised to provide the compiler with additional information for optimization decisions.

Annotations to the source code provide the compiler with specific information, usually directed at loops, so that more program parallelism may be identified. Typically, compiler directives are used to communicate this information. Compiler directives are usually comments positioned immediately before a loop. For example, the Alliant FX/80 takes advantage of these compiler directives. In the FORTRAN code displayed above, a compiler directive is inserted above the loop to inform the compiler that each element of the array K has a different value. Therefore, when the directive is added to the code,

```
cvd$        permutation(K)
      DO 5 I=1,N
   5     A(K(I)) = A(K(I)) + C(I)
```

the compiler can now easily optimize this loop for concurrent and vector execution [Alliant:88a].

Extensions. There is no standard approach for describing concurrency in an imperative language like FORTRAN, but extensions of conventional imperative languages are frequently used by supercomputer and parallel computer vendors. These language extensions are adaptations of the base language that usually focus on particular architectural features of the machine. For example, *doall* is a concurrent loop construct that allows the iterations in a piece of code to be scheduled in any order. For this reason, the following loop needs no synchronization between iterations:

```
DOALL I=1,N
      A(I) = B(I) + C(I)
      IF (A(I) >= 0) THEN
         D(I) = A(I) + 2
      END IF
END DOALL
```

The Myrias Research Corp., in fact, developed their Myrias SPS system architecture based on a programming model which involved the simple addition of one construct, *pardo* (similar to the *doall* above), to the FORTRAN language.

Library Calls. Finally, library subroutine calls are used to provide the programmer with ultimate control of concurrency and synchronization points on shared-memory machines and to provide a mechanism to send and receive messages on message-passing architectures. Typically, the use of library subroutine calls is the mechanism by which many C programs obtain concurrency on parallel architectures. The programmer can specify where parallelism exists in the code using library subroutine calls. However, the parallelism has to be explicitly specified by the programmer, and opportunities for executing code in parallel may be missed.

Illustrated below are two C processes, denoted host.c and node.c, that illustrate the use of library subroutine calls for sending and receiving messages on the Intel iPSC/2 hypercube [Intel:89].

```c
/* The code in this file (host.c) is invoked on the host.  It
 *      - allocates a group of nodes
 *      - sets the host process' PID to a known value
 *      - loads the node processes onto the cube
 *      - for each of the nodes of the cube it:
 *          - sends a message to the node
 *          - blocks on receipt of a message from the node
 *          - prints the node's message out
 */
#include <stdio.h>
#define   CUBENAME        "test"
#define   NODEPROCNAME    "node"
#define   NNODES          "4"
#define   HOSTPID         100
#define   NODEPID         0
#define   MSGTYPE         0
#define   BUFLEN          64

main()
{
    char  msgbuf[BUFLEN];       /* send/receive message buffer */
    long  msglen,               /* length of message when sending */
        nnodes = atol(NNODES),  /* number of nodes (convert string)*/
        node;                   /* node we're sending message to */

    /* allocate a given number of nodes */
    printf("Host: allocating %d nodes\n\n", nnodes);
    getcube(CUBENAME, NNODES, NULL, 1);

    /* set the Process ID of the host process to a known value */
    setpid(HOSTPID);

    /* load the node process onto all nodes with a known process id */
    load(NODEPROCNAME, -1, NODEPID);

    /* access all nodes */
    for (node=0; node<nnodes; node++){
        /* compose a message for sending */
        sprintf(msgbuf, "Hello from host...");
        /* length of message to be sent--include +1 for end of string */
        msglen = strlen(msgbuf) + 1;
        /* send message to the node */
        csend(MSGTYPE, msgbuf, msglen, node, NODEPID);
    }

    for (node=0; node<nnodes; node++){
        /* wait for receipt of next message */
        crecv(MSGTYPE, msgbuf, BUFLEN);
        /* print message out and continue */
        printf("Host: received msg: %s\n", msgbuf);
    }

    /* kill any remaining processes on cube--just to be tidy */
    killcube(-1, -1);
    /* release node allocation */
    relcube(CUBENAME);
}
```

```
/*
 * The code in this file (node.c) is loaded onto each of the nodes
 * of the cube by the host process.  The node program then:
 *     - blocks on receipt of a message from the host process
 *     - composes a message for the host
 *     - sends the message to the host
 *     - exits
 */
#define    CUBENAME "test"
#define    NNODES        "4"
#define    HOSTPID       100
#define    NODEPID       0
#define    MSGTYPE       0
#define    BUFLEN        64

main()
{
    char  msgbuf[BUFLEN];              /* send/receive message buffer */
    long  msglen,                 /* length of msg when sending */
        nnodes = atol(NNODES);    /* number of nodes in allocation */

    /* wait for receipt of next message */
    crecv(MSGTYPE, msgbuf, BUFLEN);

    /* print message out when it is received */
    printf("Node %d: received message: %s\n", mynode(), msgbuf);

    /* compose a message to send */
    sprintf(msgbuf, "Hello from node %d", mynode());

    /* length of message to be sent--include +1 for end of string */
    msglen = strlen(msgbuf) + 1;

    /* send message to the host */
    csend(MSGTYPE, msgbuf, msglen, myhost(), HOSTPID);

    printf("Node %d: process exiting...\n\n", mynode());
}
```

When the host.c program is started it loads the node.c onto all available nodes in the hypercube. The library subroutines that are used in the example are load, csend, crecv, relcube, and killcube. The host sends a message to each node. The host waits for a message from each node and prints the message on the screen. When all the nodes have responded with their messages, the host cleans out the cube. The node program waits for a starting message, then simply copies a string into a message buffer and sends the message to the host. The nodes only communicate with the host, not at all with each other. Notice for every csend, there must be a corresponding crecv.

Typically, languages for message passing machines provide library subroutines to perform both synchronous and asynchronous message passing. The above example illustrates a synchronous send and receive which is also referred to as a blocking send and receive. A program executing a blocking send or receive waits until the send is complete or the message arrives at a specified location before it continues processing. An asynchronous send or receive does not block. The status of the send or receive may be checked at a later time. For example, after a non-blocking receive is issued, the program performs other work not dependent on the message expected to be received. The program anticipates that the message will be received when it needs the information.

Summary. All four of the approaches discussed above (parallelizing compilers, annotations, language extensions, and library calls) are used to assist in executing languages on parallel computers and are very popular with parallel supercomputer and parallel computer vendors. However, these approaches have several limitations. Most important, when an application is first described in an imperative language, and when the serial code is then analyzed by the compiler or modified by the programmer, some of the inherent parallelism in the application may not be expressed in the actual parallel code. Secondly, the resulting code is usually not portable to a different parallel computer. Even in the case of a parallelizing compiler, the serial code may have been altered to allow a particular parallelizing compiler to recognize the loops that ought to be executed concurrently. These modifications to the original code may imply that it is not as portable as it once was. Finally, the resulting code is often difficult to debug. For example, most parallelizing compilers will not concurrentize a loop that has input/output statements. However, without output statements, it may be difficult to ascertain the values of variables during the execution of the loop.

Manual parallelization, using library subroutine calls, also can make debugging very challenging. For example, a misplaced call to a barrier library routine (i.e., a wait for all processors) or a missing call to a send routine (i.e., csend in node.c), when there is a corresponding call to a receive routine (i.e., crecv in host.c) waiting, are common programming errors that are difficult to find. For these reasons, new languages and different software paradigms are fruitful areas of ongoing research. Indeed, it may be necessary to change the language or the paradigm in order to obtain the best performance [Bell:89].

3.4 New Languages and Paradigms

New languages and software paradigms allow programmers to express parallelism in a more natural way. There are many parallel programming languages available, each having its own advantages and disadvantages. These run the gamut from procedural languages with tasking capability to functional and object-oriented languages.

In this section, four different languages and paradigms are described. In particular, data flow languages, Linda, Ada, and object-oriented languages, are used as the examples of new or novel approaches to programming parallel computers. Although there are other approaches/languages for obtaining concurrency that are certainly worthy of discussion (notably, concurrent logic languages), those discussed here are currently popular and provide good examples. For each of the languages and paradigms, the discussion will include a tutorial on how the language/paradigm expresses parallelization, the commercial availability of the language/paradigm, and in what applications, in particular C^3 applications, the language/paradigm is used.

3.5 Data Flow Languages

Parallelizing compilers for imperative languages like FORTRAN attempt to identify actual data dependencies vis-a-vis the artificially imposed dependencies which are caused by the nature of these languages. This is a very difficult problem for these compilers to adequately resolve because opportunities for parallelism in imperative languages are frequently obscured. For example, programs often have loops where each iteration is either dependent on the current or a previous iteration, or is independent of all previous iterations. The compiler, however, must attempt to identify any data dependencies. For this reason, the compiler is forced to make conservative decisions and will generate sequential code if it is given no other information. These difficult situations arise partly because FORTRAN programs carry an implicit state of computation (history-sensitive) and have destructive updates (e.g., can modify a variable and change its value). Therefore, generating data flow graphs that identify all the potential parallelism in imperative languages is difficult because only the most obvious parallelism will be represented.

Programs written in a data flow language, on the other hand, can be directly translated into data flow graphs that identify all the inherent parallelism in the algorithm. Each data flow graph is a directed graph in which nodes represent functions or operations and each arrow or arc between nodes represents data dependencies. Data flow graphs provide a visual representation that makes all data dependencies explicit. Data flow graphs are the machine language of data flow computers. The parallelism exposed using data flow graphs and data flow languages resides at the instruction level and is referred to as fine-grain parallelism.

Data flow languages are actually an off-shoot of functional languages and, therefore, are similar in nature. Functional languages carry out computations by the application of functions, i.e., the evaluation of expressions. Writing programs in a functional language is similar to writing mathematical equations. Advocates of functional languages believe that the concise form of these programs, coupled with their mathematical foundations, allow these programs to be proved correct by mathematical analysis, thereby leading to error-free software.

Tutorial. To illustrate the utility of data flow graphs, let's begin by examining a typical FORTRAN code segment where each statement has an identifying label:

```
1: P = X + Y
2: Q = P / Y
3: R = X * P
4: S = R - Q
5: T = R * P
6: U = S/T
```

To produce this code, a programmer has to make arbitrary decisions regarding the ordering of some of these statements. For example, it is immaterial whether statement 2 is executed before or after statement 3 as far as the intended algorithm is concerned. Similarly, the ordering of statements 4 and 5 is also arbitrary.

In figure 3-1, the data flow graph for the previous FORTRAN example clearly shows which statements can be executed concurrently. Data flow graph nodes are said to *fire* when there is data or a *token* at each of its incoming arcs. Therefore, more than one node may fire at a time. After the input tokens are absorbed, and the function or operation is executed, the result (new token) is placed on all outgoing arcs to be sent to other nodes. In the previous example, when node 4 receives tokens from node 3 (result R) and node 2 (result Q) it can fire, placing result S on the arc toward node 6. The parallelism hidden in the FORTRAN code segment can be clearly seen in the data flow graph. After the node 1 operations have been completed and a token (or result P) is placed on its outgoing arcs (to nodes 2, 3, and 5), node 2 and node 3 can fire concurrently. Similarly node 5 can fire after node 3 is completed and node 4 fires after node 2 processes its input and generates a result. In other words, a node can fire as soon as all the data that is needed at that node is made available.

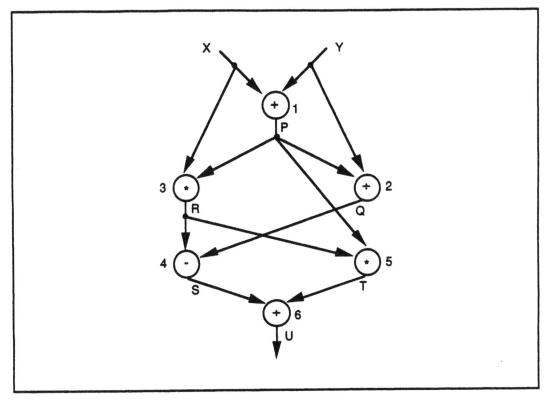

Figure 3-1. Data Flow Graph

Analysis of the data flow graph shown in figure 3-1 [Hwang:84, Ackerman:82] identifies two opportunities (nodes 2,3 and nodes 4,5) for concurrent execution of nodes. Moreover, this data flow graph explicitly shows all the parallelism inherent in the FORTRAN code and, equally important, no other data dependencies. For this reason, the graph depicts only a partial ordering of operations while the FORTRAN code imposes a complete, though arbitrary, ordering of the operations sequence.

Data flow languages/graphs can be thought of in terms of mathematical functions; programs written in a data flow language contain no notion of implicit present state, program counter, or storage. Referring back to the previous FORTRAN example, if the code for statement 2 has just been executed, then values for variables P and Q have been stored in memory. In addition, the program counter is pointing to statement 3, but statement 3 has not yet been executed. The value of R stored in memory is either undefined or has an assigned value from an earlier calculation. Thus, the present state, program counter, and values in storage of the calculation are clearly known. However, in the data flow graph, after node 2 has completed firing, the only fact that can be concluded about data on the arcs or about the nodes is directly related to the actual data dependencies shown in the graph. For example, if node 2 has just completed firing, then node 1 had to have fired at least once. There is no present state, storage, or program counter. These concepts are meaningless in the context of the data flow graph. The information necessary to perform the algorithm is expressed in the graph by virtue of the arcs, nodes, and the tokens. At first data flow languages may seem frightening to programmers accustomed to conventional programming techniques, but, in fact, it is just those features of an imperative language that make writing code for parallel processors much more difficult.

The following example Id code computes the inner product of two vectors, A and B.

```
def ip A B =
   { s = 0.0
   in  { for i <- 1 to n do
         next s = s + A[i] * B[i]
         finally s }};
```

At first glance the Id code looks similar to the functionally equivalent FORTRAN code.

```
      S = 0.0
      DO 10 I = 1,N
         S = S + A(I) * B(I)
   10 CONTINUE
```

However, the Id and FORTRAN models of computation are different in two important ways.

In the FORTRAN model, the variables "S" and "I" correspond to memory locations that are updated during each iteration. Therefore, the model assumes that only one iteration will execute at a time. The variables "s" and "i" in the Id model do not correspond to memory locations. For example, at the completion of the Id loop there will be n+1 "s" variables where the final value of "s" corresponds to the value of the function ip.

Moreover, in the FORTRAN model, the assumption is that the iterations are computed one at a time, in order from 1 to N. While in the Id model, the assumption is that all n iterations will be started simultaneously and executed concurrently. The only limit is the data dependencies of the computation itself. In this example, the only data dependency is the computation of the next "s" based on a previous "s". However, the n multiplications are not dependent on "s" and, therefore, can be computed in any order or concurrently.

Availability. Computer architectures have been developed specifically to execute data flow languages with the above functional concepts. These data flow computers are based on the concept of data-driven scheduling and computation; that is, operations are executed as soon as their operands are available. The sequence of operations to be executed is based on the data dependencies in the program. Since data flow languages typically translate into data flow graphs, data flow languages are ideally matched to data flow computers.

Although data flow languages were not originally created for von Neumann architectures (computers that store programs and data in memory and that use a program counter to control the execution of instructions), there are compilers for data flow languages that operate on von Neumann machines. However, these implementations may be inefficient, because von Neumann machines are not well adapted to support functional concepts that give rise to potential problems involving overhead and memory storage (i.e., time versus space). For example, because data flow languages do not have destructive updating, new copies of variables are created whenever the value of the variable must be modified. This means that the overhead to manipulate the variables and the number of variables rapidly increases. More powerful attributes of data flow languages also exacerbate the time versus space trade-off. Similarly, data flow language implementations for parallel non-data flow machines can exhibit other problems of overhead associated with scheduling, executing, and completing a task.

A highly visible disadvantage of data flow languages is that the attributes of these languages also make for slower execution speeds. These include the high frequency of function calls, garbage collection overhead, lack of destructive updating, and recursion. However, compiler techniques to improve the efficiency of these languages by reducing overhead problems associated with function calls, garbage collection, and recursion are active areas of ongoing research.

Some functional languages are many years old, while others are still evolving or have only recently appeared. These languages have a strong foothold in academic circles, but are not yet widely used in commercial contexts. For this reason, they still tend to be viewed as experimental. However, several parallel computers have been designed to execute data flow and functional languages efficiently; one such machine, the Monsoon, executes the data flow language Id [Arvind:90]. A Monsoon prototype was delivered to the Massachusetts Institute of Technology (MIT) this past spring by Motorola, Inc. It is a 16-node system and is capable of processing up to 10 million tokens per second. It will be used for experimenting with data flow concepts [Herbst:91].

In addition, there are other efforts underway to place data flow and functional languages onto commercial parallel-processing machines. For example, Sisal is a data flow language that is currently implemented on commercial parallel-processing machines such as the Sequent, Encore, Cray, and the Alliant. In addition, a new language called Haskell has recently been developed [Hudak:89]. Haskell is a general-purpose, purely functional programming language that contains the latest modern programming features. Besides having a potential to be a functional language standard, it is intended to operate on parallel computers.

Some recent performance data on Sisal may be of interest; this data appeared in [Cann:91]. In the table, Sisal and FORTRAN on the Cray X-MP/48 (concurrent-vector) are compared on three benchmarks. The first table shows run-time in seconds. The second table shows memory image size in kilowords.

Table 1. Run-time in Seconds

Program	One CPU		Four CPUs	
	Sisal	FORTRAN	Sisal	FORTRAN
Richard	0.39	0.35	0.14	0.11
Simple	13.52	13.49	4.90	12.37
Weather	5.93	13.92	1.84	13.51

Table 2. Memory Image Size in Kilowords

Program	Sisal	FORTRAN
Richard	93.8	113.4
Simple	544.2	406.0
Weather	566.0	163.9

These data suggest that the traditionally sluggish performance of functional languages can be substantially improved by modern compiler techniques—perhaps even to the point where they are competitive with imperative languages. If so, they may come to offer attractive advantages for use on parallel computers, because there are no hidden data dependencies to obstruct parallelization of the code.

Applications. One question that might be asked is what types of problems are solved using functional and data flow languages. The general answer is that these languages are good for solving problems that require potentially thousands of tasks running concurrently. In addition, these languages are good for a programmer who seeks a more natural way to describe complex problems which are to be automatically run concurrently. In particular, the Computational Structures Group at MIT has used the language Id running on a data flow simulator to solve dynamic programming problems, partial differential equations, Monte Carlo simulations, and simulated annealing problems.

Functional languages and data flow languages are being used in other ways as well. They can be used for writing system specifications [Burton:88]. These specifications are executable and can be verified through the use of mathematics. Data flow languages have been used at MITRE for simulating neural networks and for prototyping algorithms [Smotroff:90]. Furthermore, new task partitions of applications for eventual parallel execution on different target machines can be identified by exposing the inherent parallelism of the application [Michaud:91]. At MITRE, techniques are being developed to aid in architecture-independent parallel programming by parsing algorithm data flow graphs. The data flow graphs are then annotated with cost models. Improved architecture-specific cost metrics which reflect architectural characteristics such as contention and saturation are being developed to guide in the development of the actual partition [Gill:89, 90].

Summary. Data flow languages provide a mechanism that implicitly captures the inherent parallelism of an application program and, therefore, frees the programmer from concerns of synchronization and interprocessor communication. Data flow languages may be a vehicle to more fully take advantage of computational power that exists in today's parallel computers, as well as the supercomputers of the future.

3.6 Linda

Linda is a parallel-programming paradigm that was first described by D. Gelernter in 1982 at Yale University [Gelernter:88]. Linda basically is a library that is called from existing languages (i.e., C and FORTRAN) to implement concurrent tasks. As parallel machines become the wave of the present, tools are increasingly needed to assist programmers in creating parallel tasks and coordinating their activities. Linda was designed to be such a tool. Linda was designed with three important goals in mind: to be portable, efficient, and easy to use.

Tutorial. The fundamental concept behind Linda is relatively simple: information to be shared by multiple programs or multiple processes is placed in a memory area called a *tuple space* (TS). The data items themselves are called *tuples*. TS is like an associative memory, since tuples are selected on the basis of an element-by-element match rather than by using a specific address. A tuple is an ordered sequence of data items. For example, the tuple ("smith", 50, true) contains three data items: a string, an integer and a boolean.

Linda performs the following four primitive operations on tuple space:

    out   place a tuple in TS

    in   match a tuple and remove it from TS

    rd   match a tuple and return a copy of it

    eval   create a live tuple (a new process).

For example, the operation *out* ("smith", 50, true) generates the tuple ("smith", 50, true) and places it into TS where it becomes available to other processes. In figure 3-2, the operation *out* ("smith", 50, true) adds this tuple to tuple space while the operation *in* ("smith", ? age, ? married) withdraws a matching tuple from tuple space. The operation *rd* ("smith", ? age, ? married) reads a matching tuple without removing it. Because there is no synchronization necessary between the process doing the *out* and the process (or processes) doing the *rd* or *in*, the *out* operation is never suspended or blocked; therefore, the process that elicited it continues immediately. In addition, there can exist any number of copies of the same tuple in TS.

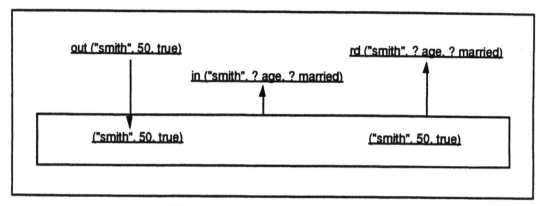

Figure 3-2. Tuple Space Example

Tuples in TS are accessed by matching them against a pattern field. The parameters denoting the tuple can be expressed by either *actuals* (a value) or *formals* (a variable). *Actuals* are matched exactly and *formals* must match a value of the same type. For example, the operation

```
int age;
boolean married;
in ('smith', ?age, ?married);
```

will match any tuple in TS whose first field is the string "smith", and whose second and third fields are an integer and a boolean, respectively. Here "smith" is an actual because it is a string, and *age* and *married* are formals. In this case, the important key is the string "smith", and the tuple that it matches is ("smith", 50, true). That is, *age* is assigned 50 and *married* is assigned true, and then the tuple is removed from TS.

If there is nothing in TS that matches the tuple, then the current process is suspended until a match is made. (Linda also provides functions that return false when no match is found rather than suspending the process.) On the other hand, if multiple tuples are matched, then which one to choose is an arbitrary decision. It then becomes the programmer's problem to keep track of the multiple tuples that are being dumped into tuple space. An extra field, for example, could be added to the tuples to keep them in order.

All of these types of tuples are called *passive tuples*. There is no operation that can modify a tuple in place, as in conventional languages. In order to modify a tuple, the tuple must be physically removed from TS by way of an *in*, then it can be modified and placed back into TS using the *out* operation. This ensures complete protection from overwriting the variable, eliminating the need for semaphores or monitors for protecting the variable. While tuples can be of any size, the original Linda paradigm does not provide for indirect addressing (e.g., arrays). Instead, complex data structures can be created by means of the operator *eval*.

The operator *eval* is like the operator *out*, except that *eval* creates a *live tuple*, whose fields are not evaluated until after the tuple enters TS. For example, if *fmar* is a function, then the operation *eval* ("smith", 50, fmar(x)) creates a new process (a live tuple) to evaluate the function fmar(x), which runs in parallel with the calling process. *Eval* implicitly forks a new process to perform the evaluation. A live tuple is created which is independent of, and can be executed in parallel with, the task which created it. When the process is completed, the resulting (passive) tuple is left in TS, as if an *out* had created it. To create multiple parallel processes, multiple *evals* can be issued. In this way, dynamic tasking becomes a reality and programmers can build any kind of data structures they need out of tuples.

A complex data structure, for example, can be created in TS by creating different processes for each part of the structure. An example of this type of a program might be one whose result is an N by N matrix. Each element of the result can be expressed by using multiple *evals* as in the following C-Linda code segment:

```
{
    int i,j,max;
    for (i=0; i<=max; ++i)
        for (j=0; j<=max; ++j)
            eval ("M", i, j, compute(i,j));   /*fork process */
}
```

As soon as each compute(i,j) process is completed, it turns into a passive tuple and becomes the element in the i-th row and j-th column of the matrix identified by "M", all of which is located in TS. Each element of the matrix becomes visible to all processes as soon as it becomes a passive tuple.

Using Linda operations, the programmer can send a message from one process/processor to another without worrying about the underlying architecture and without worrying about the other process. Tuple space is conceptually both shared and global, and communication through it is possible between processes at any time. Processes need to know nothing about each other. They do not need to know where the message is coming from or where it is going. Since the compiler does most of the work of communication and synchronization, it is easier to program in this manner. Since the processes are loosely connected, the programmer can more easily develop each module independently from the rest. It is the Linda implementation rather than the programmer that deals with the physical distribution of the data.

Most Linda implementations contain both a run-time kernel and a preprocessor or a compiler. The kernel is language-independent, and it manages the processes and implements interprocess communication. Because the tuple space concept requires a great deal of searching on each operation, a preprocessor is usually used for facilitating the run-time search. The preprocessor analyzes the various Linda operations and divides them into groups according to the type of tuple space access. For example, *ins* and *rd*s are matched with *out*s and *eval*s (and vice versa) and placed into groups based on matching tuple patterns. They are then mapped onto the appropriate family of routines in the run-time library.

Availability. The Linda system has been implemented on several different computer architectures. Two of them, the S/Net Linda kernel and the VAX-Network Linda kernel, are on distributed systems. The two systems, however, are implemented very differently. The S/Net version relies on an *out* being broadcast to all nodes, whereas the VAX implementation is the inverse. An *out* is a local command but an *in* is broadcast. Another Linda kernel, for the Intel iPSC hypercube, relies on point-to-point communication where tuple space is implemented as distributed hash tables that scale with machine size. Systems have also been written for the Encore, Sequent, and Alliant shared-memory machines which run much faster and are also much simpler than the network types. An S/Net-like architecture called the *Linda Machine*, with hardware that supports tuple space operations, is under construction at AT&T Bell Laboratories. In addition, Linda is commercially available from Scientific Computing Associates of New Haven, CT, for the Encore and Sequent shared-memory machines. A group at Yale distributes a simulator for Sun workstations.

There are development and debugging tools available for Linda. At Yale University, a tuple space visualization tool has been developed called TupleScope. It is a mouse-driven tool that displays a "snapshot" of the state of tuple space at any given time. A series of windows is displayed, each one tagged with a separate tuple class, and within each window, each tuple in the class is depicted by a sphere. The contents of a specific tuple can be displayed by selecting with a mouse the particular sphere. According to Carriero, this tuple space visualization tool promises to be a valuable debugging tool [Carriero:89]. There is also an emacs-based editor called Linda Program Builder [Ahmed:91].

The Linda paradigm has a number of advantages for the applications programmer. First, it is easy to use, because the four basic operations are simple to understand, and they are designed to be used in conjunction with established languages. Also, they deal easily with process creation and with communication and synchronization by way of the tuple space concept. Secondly, Linda clearly expresses parallel data structures by way of live tuples, which is a very natural way for the programmer to conceptualize them. Since the implementation is transparent to the programmer, Linda's uncoupled approach to programming in parallel facilitates the programmer's communication job and minimizes his interaction with the operating system. Thirdly, because the programming model is not tied to the underlying architecture, it is portable even between shared and distributed-memory machines.

On the other hand, Linda has its disadvantages. Because Linda is such a high-level programming model, its efficiency relies heavily on the efficiency of the particular Linda kernel implementation. The tuple matching process can be slow, depending on the type of machine and the implementation. In addition, because multiple tuples can be matched in tuple space and because the order of Linda operations is not guaranteed, the burden remains on the programmer to use the tuple space concept with care. Critics of Linda are not convinced that it has any advantages over traditional message-oriented systems or monitors, and they fear that Linda's lack of synchronization is potentially dangerous [Davidson:89].

Applications. Cogent Research, producers of transputer-based parallel workstations, have implemented a version of Linda called Kernel Linda. Their parallel-operating system, QIX, uses Kernel Linda for interprocess communication, and Kernel Linda is also available for applications programming. Cogent Research has also implemented Kernel Linda bindings for C, C^{++}, and FORTRAN.

Linda is currently in use at MITRE in the Joint Message Analysis and Processing System (JMAPS) project. MITRE implemented an object-oriented version of Linda that uses shared memory. The design extends Linda to handle complex structures, or objects, in addition to fundamental data types. It also handles multiple tuple spaces and tuple spaces within tuple spaces. Linda operations are employed as the only means of interprocess communication in a logically and physically distributed system. In the JMAPS design, a Linda tuple space is regarded as a general-purpose, concurrent, first-class persistent naming environment (a view adopted from symmetric programming [Jagannathan:89]), and, as such, tuple spaces are used in many capacities. To improve accessibility, all system-wide information is stored in a global tuple space used as a distributed-file system.

It has been found that the use of Linda extensions, combined with the object-oriented approach, has been easy to implement, and in addition, the project was easier to conceptualize. In actuality, however, the movement of large data structures and arrays can be inefficient. The investigation into issues such as efficiency and fault tolerance has just begun.

Summary. Linda is still in its infancy. More tools are needed, and more machine environments and language models need to be tested, but Linda's developers are confident that true progress is being made to that end.

3.7 Ada

Ada is the standard programming language of the Department of Defense (DOD) [DOD:83]. Originally created to meet the programming needs of DOD-embedded computer systems, Ada was designed to support software engineering principles for programming large real-time systems. This language, specified jointly by academia, industry, and government, from its inception, incorporated important software engineering principles and features of languages popular in the early 1970s: to create reliable, maintainable, efficient, and understandable software. As a result, Ada was designed to support the evolution and maintenance of reusable, portable, and real-time software [DSB:87].

Most important to our discussion is the fact that Ada was designed from its inception to be able to run tasks concurrently. Ada is the first widely accepted programming language with its own model of concurrency. This permits the application programmer to write portable concurrent programs. Ada achieves concurrency through the *tasking* model. A task is an Ada program unit that contains a separate sequence of instructions that may be executed concurrently with other tasks. Tasks were designed to be executed on multiprocessor systems, or time-sliced on a uniprocessor machine. Since the number of processors on parallel computers may be less than the number of tasks, it is important that Ada was designed with the capability to map available computational resources to logical tasks.

Tutorial. A task, like other Ada program units (e.g., subprograms) is defined by a specification and a body. In general, a specification identifies and describes the visible information, specifies which information may be used, and describes how it may be used. The body contains the code that actually performs these functions. In a task specification, however, only the entry points into the task are defined and, in fact, the task entries look like procedures. Ada's task declarations cannot stand alone as separate compiler units; they have to be nested inside a parent unit such as a block statement. The reasons for this have to do with the rules that define a task's activation and termination. Every Ada task has a master and tasks are activated when the task's body is elaborated[1] at the end of the declarative part of the master program unit (i.e., task activation is implicit). Once the master's elaboration is complete, the task can start to run.

There are complex rules for terminating tasks, but suffice to say that a task terminates when it has completed its work and when all subordinate tasks have been terminated. Ada permits tasks to be created on the fly, which makes the rules for task masters and

---

[1] In Ada terminology declarations are *elaborated*, statements are *executed*, and expressions are *evaluated* [Wegner:80]. The elaboration of a task body makes the body come into existence and from then on it may be executed.

task termination more complex, but their basic concept of dependence on the master task holds.

Tasks without any entries run independently of each other and have no explicit synchronization with other tasks. There is implicit synchronization with the task master, in that the master may not exit until the task has terminated. Tasks without entries represent a good paradigm for divide and conquer type problems, but they are not powerful enough to solve many other types of problems, as will be described later. For this reason, Ada provides a more sophisticated and encompassing synchronization mechanism. The *rendezvous*, a form of remote procedure call, is the Ada mechanism for task coordination and for sharing of information. A rendezvous occurs when one task calls an entry in the other task, and the receiving task is prepared to accept the entry. Rendezvous is best explained by comparing it to a telephone. One person calls another person. The phone rings (and the caller is blocked) until the recipient answers the phone. It is possible that the recipient is sitting by his phone waiting for it to ring. Once the phone rings and the recipient answers, the two tasks are in a rendezvous. When the rendezvous (phone call) is over, the two tasks proceed independently.

It is important to note that callers of a given task entry are queued in first-in, first-out order. In addition, each task may have a priority. Priorities are used only to indicate relative degrees of urgency and are given to assist the implementation in the allocation of processing resources to parallel tasks. The end result is that the highest priority tasks execute when the resources they require become available. Scheduling, using priorities, therefore, is preemptive. However, priorities are not to be used for task synchronization. The structure of the actual Ada code is asymmetric in that the rendezvous or entry point is declared in one task, not both tasks. An example task specification (which shows only the code segments of interest) is shown below:

```
task T1;            -- specification of task 1
task T2 is          -- specification of task 2
     entry E;       -- entry declaration
end;
```

In this example, an entry named E is declared in task T2 (similar to declaring a variable, I, an integer in a FORTRAN program). There is no entry declared in task T1. However, the body of task T1 has an *entry call* statement. In task T1's body, the entry call looks like a procedure invocation and is T1's rendezvous (synchronization) point.

```
task body T1 is         -- body of task 1
   ...
begin
   ...
   T2.E;                -- entry call
   ...
end;
```

Moreover, T2's task body contains the *accept* statement which specifies the actions to be performed. Within T2's task body, the accept statement does not name the task (in this case, T1) but it does name the entry point, as illustrated below. This allows tasks other than T1 to have entry calls to E in T2. Since accept statements do not name the task whose entry call is to be accepted, these service tasks can be designed as general-purpose utilities similar to subprograms.

```
task body T2 is    --  body of task 2
    ...
begin
    ...
    accept E do       -- accept statement
                .
                .
                .
    end;
        ...
end;
```

The above example of an entry call (E) was actually an unconditional entry call because the calling task (T1) unconditionally waits until the called task (T2) accepts the call. Entry calls can be either unconditional, conditional, or timed. One of the most commonly used facilities is the conditional entry call which attempts an immediate rendezvous. If the rendezvous is not immediately possible, the caller is not queued, and the processing continues with the next statement. A timed entry call is executed when the called tasks accept the entry call within a specified time value.

Another facility, the Ada select statement, is used to choose entries nondeterministically from a set of outstanding requests. The called task may use a selective-wait statement to accept any one of a number of alternatives. Guards (conditional tests) in front of the select alternatives provide further control.

The Ada tasking model with the rendezvous mechanism supports the implementation of many classical concurrency paradigms. In general, applications that have a need for concurrent actions, routing messages, managing shared resources, and interrupt handling can be implemented using the tasking mechanism. More specifically, a rendezvous can serve as a semaphore protecting a section of code. Different scheduling than first-in-first-out queues can be implemented by using entry families. Finally, tasking paradigms (such as monitors and barriers) and synchronization protocols (such as gates and self-scheduling for-loops) can also be implemented in terms of the Ada task structure.

Ada also possesses many other features that are useful for solving problems requiring concurrent processing. For example, Ada allows for families of entries to ensure ordered regular interaction among tasks.

Availability. The Ada Joint Program Office (AJPO) is responsible for maintaining a stable Ada language definition. The AJPO accomplishes this task by applying the criteria specified in the Ada Programming Language document to validate that a given Ada compiler conforms to its standards. In the past, compilers that received a validation certificate from the AJPO could use the DOD's trademark Ada name, but Ada has recently become public software and no longer carries the DOD trademark. All validated compilers implement the full language. However, Ada validation does not guarantee that code generated by the compiler will meet performance requirements or be suitable for a particular application.

Ada is a complex, sophisticated language. The Ada language, however, continues to evolve through two well-controlled procedures called commentaries and revisions. A commentary is an official interpretation of the Ada standard that has been approved by the Director of the AJPO. These commentaries meet ANSI requirements and are approved by the International Standards Organization [SigAda:89]. The Ada 9X Project is responsible for revising and updating the Ada standard. During 1989, revision requests were submitted by interested people in the Ada community. These revision requests will form the basis for a revised language-requirements document and the language revision itself. Alternative methods for real-time scheduling, object-oriented programming, fixed-point arithmetic, and implementation dependencies affecting performance predictability are some of the issues under discussion [AdaIC:90a].

Many validated Ada compilers and associated support tools are currently available. For example, 272 base compilers and 133 derived compilers have been validated by the AJPO as of 1 May 1990 [AdaIC:90b]. Once a compiler has been validated, the vendor will typically spend time improving its execution speed and quality. Many of the validated compilers are specifically designed for parallel computers and supercomputers. For example, there are compilers for the Alliant FX/80, CONVEX, Cray X-MP, Encore Multimax 320, iPSC/2 Parallel Supercomputer, and Sequent Symmetry.

There are many advantages to using the Ada programming language. Ada was specifically designed to support the evolution and maintenance of reusable, portable, and real-time software. Ada was designed from the beginning to support concurrent tasks on multiprocessor systems. The concurrent task feature was not added on as an afterthought. Validated Ada compilers exist on many different machines.

On the other hand, there are a few disadvantages in using the Ada programming language for parallel processing. Although the concepts of the rendezvous and the tasking model are very powerful, these concepts do not match any specific parallel-hardware architecture well. Secondly, the semantics of the Ada language often give automatic code parallelizers difficulty. In particular, parallel processes and exceptions (predefined or user-defined error conditions, such as, divide by zero) do not interact very well. It is at times difficult to produce the same results with parallel processing as the comparable serial code when an exception occurs on one of the parallel processes. Finally, Ada does require a significant learning curve in order to take full advantage of the capabilities that it offers for parallel processing.

The Ada tasking model maps easily to uniprocessor and shared-memory multiprocessor architectures. On the other hand, Ada is more challenging to implement on distributed systems. Writing code in any general-purpose language (FORTRAN, C, or Ada) for execution on distributed systems is difficult because the specific-target-hardware configuration usually has to be heavily factored into early design activities. Researchers are actively investigating different approaches to distribute an Ada program across multiple machines.

MITRE has several on-going research efforts investigating Ada concurrency and run time issues. For example, MITRE has developed a distributed simulation for the Strategic Defense Initiative (SDI) program to study SDI effectiveness as a function of space-based platform architecture and battle-management algorithms. The simulation is called the Experimental Version Prototype (EVP) and contains roughly 20,000 lines of Ada code. The simulation code incorporates many of Ada's advanced capabilities. MITRE originally developed the simulation on a DEC VAX and on Sun Workstation computers and then ported the simulation to the three different shared-memory parallel machines built by Encore, Alliant, and Sequent to test the model [Bensley:88a].

MITRE personnel also participate in Ada professional and standards organizations. One of the more important issues that the MITRE Ada Speciality Group is involved with, through the Association for Computing Machinery SigAda working groups, involves the question of real-time processing. The Ada tasking paradigm evolved in part to meet real-time programming requirements of the 1970s and was not designed to meet contemporary standards for flexible scheduling strategies and priorities in real-time programming environments. To overcome this limitation, researchers have developed a variety of approaches for improving the real-time performance of Ada applications. The MITRE Ada speciality group also works with the Ada 9X committee to document and define changing requirements for the language.

Applications. Several large Air Force systems are using Ada. An impressive example of an Ada program is the TRW Defense Systems Group's Command Center Processing and Display Segment Replacement (CCPDS-R) system at Cheyenne Mountain. The Preliminary Design Review demonstration consisted of 130 Ada tasks executing on a network of three VAX nodes [Royce:89, Royce:90]. This interconnection of tasks required 450 task-to-task interfaces.

TRW used a message-based paradigm with buffers to build the Network Architecture Services (NAS) to handle interprocessor communication between Ada programs running on different processors. NAS is implemented in an Ada environment and uses operating-system services to implement inter- and intra-processor communication. NAS is a distributed executive and CCPDS-R uses NAS as a building block. These building blocks are integrated with application interfaces to develop demonstrations.

Several other new programs using Ada have recently been awarded by the Air Force. These include the Icelandic Air Defense System (IADS), and the E-3 Radar System Improvement Program (RSIP) upgrade to the Airborne Warning and Control System (AWACS). IADS will operate on a VAX connected to workstations that function as display consoles for the operators. RSIP will operate on a four-processor militarized MIPS computer system. Separate Ada programs will execute on each processor concurrently. Communication between processors will be handled by the operating system using message passing. Finally, Ada is also being employed in system upgrades of the COBRA DANE System Modernization (CDSM), a ground-based, large-scale phased array radar.

Summary. Ada is the first widely accepted programming language with its own model of concurrency as well as one which encourages sound software engineering practices. Ada is being used in several DOD programs for implementing real-time embedded systems and many commercial projects. More compilers are being validated with a special emphasis on Ada compilers for multiprocessor machines. As the technology in hardware and compiler design continues to improve, Ada may become one of the most important software environments for multiprocessor machines for parallel processing applications.

3.8 Object-Oriented Languages

Object-oriented programming is a style of programming that has been popular in the computer simulation and artificial intelligence communities for some time. Lately it is beginning to gain favor among commercial software developers because of the modularity and code reusability it provides for software development. It is also believed by some of the leading multicomputer system researchers and designers, Seitz at Caltech, Hewitt and Dally at MIT, to be a good model of computation for distributed memory message passing systems.

Object-oriented programming traces its roots to Simula-67, an object-oriented simulation language [Kreutzer:86]. Smalltalk-80, developed at Xerox PARC [Goldberg:83], is a purely object-oriented language and program development environment. Flavors and CLOS are object-oriented extensions to Common Lisp [Keene:88]. C++ [Lippman:89, Stroustrup:87] and Objective C [Cox:86] are object-oriented extensions to the C language. Actors [Agha:86] is an object-oriented model for concurrent systems developed by Hewitt of MIT and Agha of Yale University. In the literature, the term "actors" is frequently used to mean concurrent objects, that is, objects that are independent in the sense that they may execute code concurrently. Cantor [Athas:89] is an object-oriented language that is being developed at Caltech to be used on Seitz's Mosaic 16,000 processor multicomputer. Seitz was one of the original designers of the hypercube topology. CST is a Smalltalk-80 based concurrent programming language being developed at MIT to be used on Dally's J-Machine [Dally:89].

Tutorial. The model of computation is the programmer's view of the machine. It is the model he uses to develop his program. In the computational model of traditional top-down development, data and control functions are separate, as for example in FORTRAN programming. The programmer determines the data structures and functionally decomposes the problem into a set of subroutines that operate on the data structures.

In the object-oriented model of computation, the data and control functions are encapsulated in self-contained program units called *objects*. These objects communicate with each other by sending messages. An object can be likened to a real-world entity. It has a state that it maintains, represented by *instance variables*, which are memory locations. It responds to stimuli, represented by the messages it receives. It exhibits behaviors in response to the messages it receives, represented by *methods*, which are sets of program instructions.

The commercially supported object-oriented languages, such as Smalltalk and C++, allow a programmer to define different types or classes of objects. A class definition includes the source code definition of the instance variables and the message/method pairs associated with every instance of the class. Inheritance is supported, that is, classes may be defined as refinements of other classes (for example, a savings account is a special kind of bank account). Multiple inheritance allows a class to be defined as a refinement of two or more classes.

In many traditional programming languages, associating or binding a variable to a certain type (for example, integer, float, savings_account) is done at the time a program is compiled. *Polymorphism* is the ability of a variable to refer at run-time to instances of different classes [Meyer:88]. Many object oriented programming languages restrict polymorphism to the class hierarchy. Suppose savings_account is a subclass or refinement of the bank_account class. It is convenient at times to be able to use the idea that an instance of savings_account is also an instance of bank_account. For example, suppose a program needs to maintain a list of all the bank accounts, some of which are savings accounts.

Dynamic binding is the ability to decide at run-time which operation to apply to a variable depending on its type. Suppose that different methods have been defined for printing savings accounts and bank accounts. If a print message is sent to every bank_account on the list, then those accounts that are in the subclass savings_account would print as a savings_account, while those that are only in the class bank_account would use the print method defined for a bank_account. These features of object-oriented languages are what make them different from many traditional programming languages. However, there are other features of object-oriented programming that makes it a good model of computation for parallel programming.

Object-oriented programming is a good model of computation for distributed-memory multicomputers, because it minimizes global information and because it provides natural communication and synchronization boundaries. In programming for a multicomputer, it is a good idea to assign to the same processor data items and code that will be used together. When writing an object-oriented program, the programmer divides the data and the functions to control that data up into objects. A side effect of this assignment is that data and functions that are frequently used together are identified. Thus, object-oriented programming facilitates the mapping of software to hardware. Most importantly, these features are a natural part of the object-oriented programming model of computation.

Mapping object-oriented programs onto parallel processors is usually done by associating instances of objects with processors. When a C++ or Smalltalk object-oriented program is executed on a sequential machine, the execution of a method that sends a message is suspended until the message sent has been completely processed. For example, suppose while object A is executing a method, A sends a message to object B. At this point A's method execution is suspended until B has completely executed the method associated with its message. In sequential object-oriented programming only one method is executing (that is, one message is being processed) at a given time. In parallel object-oriented programming, many objects execute methods at the same time. Generally this is accomplished by extending the basic object-oriented message passing model to allow objects to continue executing after they have sent a message.

ABCL/1, a concurrent object-oriented language developed by Yonezawa of the Tokyo Institute of Technology [Yonezawa:87], extends the basic object-oriented message passing to allow the programmer to manage message communication using blocking and non-blocking sends. Objects maintain queues of messages that are waiting to be processed to support these extensions. The reader may recall that distributed-memory machines such as the iPSC/2 and the Symult support both blocking and non-blocking sends and receives, and each processor maintains a queue of messages on behalf of its processes.

ABCL/1 supports priority and guarded messages to control synchronization. Whether real-time programming is an issue in a particular application or not, there are times when it is useful for an object to process messages on a priority basis. For example, the programmer may wish to start a number of computations going but is only interested in a subset of the results. When this subset is obtained it may be desirable to stop the other computations from continuing so as not to waste resources. Priority messages are useful for handling these exceptional situations.

There are certain situations where the programmer may want or need to allow an object to process a certain type of message before another type of message. Typed messages (or *guarded* messages) are part of Hoare's Concurrent Sequential Processes model [Hoare:78]. They are supported in the Ada tasking model as described in a previous section. For example, suppose we have a set of objects that are producing items of information and another object that is consuming them. Because the rate of producing and consuming may be quite different, a buffer object might be used to hold items until the consumer is ready to process the next one. The buffer cannot accept a consume message if it has no items to process, but it can accept one as soon as it receives the next produce message. Similarly, the buffer cannot accept a produce message if the buffer is full, but it can accept one as soon as it receives the next consume message. To support guarded messages, a means of selectively accepting messages must be provided by the run-time system. This is usually done by providing a message queue associated with each object.

Futures are used in the Actor concurrent object-oriented model developed by Hewitt and Agha. They act as placeholders for the result of a computation. They allow one or more threads of a computation to continue until the actual value of another computation is required. In this way, they provide what is called *data-driven concurrency*. Before an object sends a message, it creates a future. When the object sends the message, it includes the location of the future in the message. When the receiving object completes the computation associated with the message, it stores the value that is the result of its computation in the future.

For certain operations, a future may be used without knowing its actual value. For example, an object may pass the location of a future as an argument in a message to another object, or it may assign the location of the future as the value of one of its instance variables. For other operations, for example, addition, the actual value of the result of the computation may be needed. In this case, the value must be retrieved from the future that holds or will eventually hold the result of the computation. If a value is requested from a future that has not been set yet, the requesting method execution is blocked until the future can reply with the value.

To allow a computation to begin as soon as the result of another is available, the Actor model uses *continuations*. A continuation is an object that contains all the information necessary to continue a computation. In most sequential object-oriented models of execution, if method L invokes method M, then when M completes executing, it returns the result of its execution to L. If M's result is required by method N, then L invokes N passing M's result as an argument. In this way L directly coordinates the sharing of information between M and N. In a language that supports continuations, L can provide M with a means of invoking N directly, as soon as M's result is available. The advantage of continuations in a multicomputer environment is that more concurrency is possible. L can continue to execute free of the responsibility of providing coordination between M and N. N can begin executing sooner because it does not have to wait for L to coordinate.

Time Warp is a model of computation for object-oriented distributed discrete-event simulation that uses checkpoint and rollback to enforce event ordering. In Time Warp, every event message has a timestamp associated with it that indicates the simulation time at which the event is to be processed by the receiving object. Associated with each object are input and output message queues, each kept in timestamp order, as well as a current state and a stack of old states. Before a message is processed, the object's current state is pushed onto the old state stack and a new current state is allocated with a timestamp equal to the message's timestamp.

If a message that has an earlier timestamp than the current state arrives at an object, the object rolls back to a state with a timestamp that is less than or equal to the timestamp on the new message. As the object rolls back, it returns messages processed out of order to its input queue and sends *anti-messages* for those output messages that were sent as a result of processing input messages out of sequence. When rollback is complete, the object begins rolling forward by processing the new message and then reprocessing the messages that were returned to its input queue.

At MITRE, we have had several projects that were related to Time Warp. In Moving Time Window, a mechanism was developed to make Time Warp simulations more efficient [Sokol:89]. In Distributed Object-Oriented Programming, we developed the SaM synchronization manager, a generalization of the basic Time Warp synchronization mechanism, to support general purpose object-oriented programming [Prelle:90, 91, 92]. In Robust Behavior in Object-Oriented Systems, we extended the SaM synchronization manager to support fault-tolerant application processing [Bensley:88b].

Availability. The C++ is frequently implemented with a preprocessor that translates the C++ into conventional C plus support library routines. Thus, it is fairly easy for multicomputer developers to offer C++ as a language option on their machines. C++ is available on the Meiko and on the NCUBE. Although C++ is not currently available on the Intel iPSC860, Northrup Research has installed it on their system.

Applications. Object Technology Institute (OTI), based in Ottawa, Canada, is a technology transfer company. Its customers are companies that want to introduce object-oriented technology into their own companies. They provide both tools and training for object-oriented software development. Supported by the Defence Research Establishment, Ottawa, work on the testbed for Electronic Support Measures (ESM) signal processing research [Barry:87, 89] is continuing at OTI; it now consists of about 100K lines of Smalltalk. (ESM involves finding and evaluating sources of radiated electromagnetic energy for the purpose of immediate threat recognition. This application deals with a passive surveillance receiver that intercepts and analyzes radar signals.) This application includes handling hard real-time data acquisition and knowledged-based signal processing.

The ESM testbed consists of a pre-processor that captures and buffers input signals, four to six single board computers that perform the signal processing tasks, and peripherals for I/O. The testbed uses Harmony, a real-time multiprocessing kernel that supports both multiprocessing and multitasking with priorities, using lightweight tasks. It provides blocking and non-blocking send and receive primitives. Actra actors encapsulate the functions and behavior of Harmony tasks. The ESM testbed uses Actra and Objective-C. Actra is a version of Smalltalk extended to support the Actor concurrent object-oriented model. Actra is used for simulating, prototyping, monitoring, debugging, testing system software, and software development tools. Objective-C is used to code tasks with real-time performance constraints. To provide the programmer with a means to control the granularity of the actors that make up the application program, the actors (concurrent objects) in Actra may consist of lower-level objects. These lower-level objects can communicate directly with each other, but communication to the outside world is done through their actor.

Simulations represent a large class of applications that stand to gain significantly from the performance improvements promised by parallel processing. Jade Simulations International Corporation (Calgary, Canada) has a product called Sim++ [Cleary:89] based on the Time Warp distributed discrete-event simulation model developed by Jefferson [Jefferson:87]. Sim++ is written in C++. It uses a special library to support simulation constructs. Sim++ is currently available for Meiko and BBN multicomputer systems. It can also be used on a network with Sun 3, Sun 4, and HP 9000 workstations.

Sim++ has been used for a number of applied simulations. The Alberta Government Telephone Company is using Sim++ for network planning. Bell Northern Research, Ottawa, uses it for electronic CAD. The Naval Research Lab uses it for a real-time communication simulation investigating the impact of such things as varying the communication media and protocols for ship-to-ship and ship-to-shore communication.

Summary. Object-oriented programming is becoming an increasingly popular model of programming in the commercial software development community because of the modularity and code reusability it provides for software development. A number of researchers in the field of parallel system development seem to believe that object-oriented programming holds promise as a model of programming for parallel computation. If object-oriented programming comes to dominate the commercial software world, as some predict, then object-oriented programming for parallel systems will probably follow.

SECTION 4

PERFORMANCE CONSIDERATIONS

4.1 Introduction

The single most important criterion for comparing machines with respect to performance must be the class or classes of applications that are going to be run on the machine. Different applications can have different performance characteristics on different machines, or allow different implementations on the same machine. A careful analysis of the characteristics of the particular application class is, therefore, crucial to improved processing performance.

In this vein there are several questions to be considered. First, are the performance requirements of the system real-time, interactive, or batch? Secondly, is it possible to meet these requirements with the allotted processing budget? In this regard there are two factors to consider: how well does the machine perform, and how much programmer effort and expertise does it take to get the machine to perform at that level?

When purchasing a system, how money is apportioned to the various components of the system should also be considered. Is the application compute, communication, or input/output bound? If the application is compute-bound, look to maximize computing power. This may be done most effectively by maximizing the number of processors. Alternatively, it may be more worthwhile to settle for fewer processors and spend the extra money for higher-performance vector processors. If the application is communication-bound, look for fast processor-to-processor communications. For such applications, this may be the single most important performance characteristic. If the application is I/O bound, look for high-bandwidth I/O, multiple I/O channels, and multiple high-capacity secondary storage subsystems.

4.2 Performance Criteria

Peak Speed. Peak speed is used to measure a machine's performance when all of its hardware is working at its maximum theoretical rate. For example, with vector processors, assume that pipes are kept continually full. For multiprocessors, assume that all processors are kept continually busy. In reality, there are no computers currently in existence that perform at their peak speed on a sustained basis. In fact, average performance for most problems is only about 25 percent of peak [Hwang:87]. Some problems such as large matrix computations can achieve more, but most programs are not sufficiently regular in structure to achieve this. Given this caveat, the reader may find the following chart (figure 4-1) that depicts peak performance in megaflops versus time of

63

interest. The numbers in parenthesis indicate the number of processors that would be used to obtain the peak performance indicated. (The data shown in this graph was obtained from [Hwang:85], [SSS: 89], and vendor supplied information.) MITRE has a number of these parallel computers available in-house including Alliant, Ametek, Encore, iPSC, iWarp, and Sequent systems.

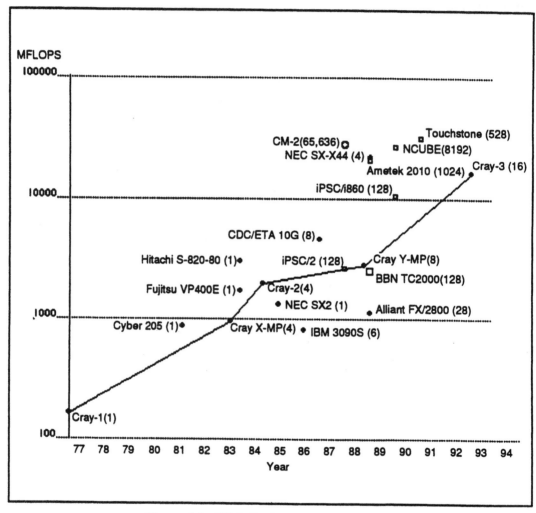

Figure 4-1. High-Performance Computing

Number of Processors. For multiprocessor systems, the number of processors is a base measure of how great a performance improvement may be obtained for appropriate applications. For certain programs, N processors may indeed yield close to a factor of N performance improvement. For communication or input/output-intensive applications, however, it may not be possible to keep those processors busy enough to obtain even 10 percent of the promised factor of N improvement. The number of processors, in any case, cannot be increased without bound; there exists a point where processor intercommunication will limit the performance benefits of more processors.

Communication Bandwidth. If processes running on different processors must communicate frequently to accomplish their work, the speed with which they can communicate and the amount of data that can be transmitted per unit time becomes a key issue. In distributed-memory systems, such as the Intel iPSC/860, the processors communicate information through message passing. If communication channels are slow, performance may be degraded when one processor must wait for data to arrive from another processor before it can continue its computation.

On shared-memory computers, communication bandwidth is generally determined by the bandwidth to the shared memory. The effective bandwidth for these systems is generally much higher than for distributed-memory systems even when the underlying hardware architecture is similar. This higher bandwidth is essential because distributed-memory systems pass general-purpose messages requiring high software overhead to process. In most cases, expensive memory allocation techniques are also employed. Shared-memory architectures, on the other hand, manipulate highly structured data, and the hardware is tailored to accommodate this, thereby eliminating or minimizing software overhead.

The topology of a multiprocessor system may affect its performance to a greater or lesser extent. If it does not take much longer to send a message between two processors that are not directly connected, compared to the time it takes to send a message between two processors that are directly connected, then the topology may have little effect on overall performance.

Load Balancing. Load balancing concerns the distribution of work among available processors. In shared-memory machines the simple expedient of allocating the next ready task to a processor that becomes idle is viable because all tasks are more or less equally available in the shared memory. If a more efficient scheme is needed, or if (as in a distributed-memory system) all tasks are not equally available, the programmer is usually responsible for deciding how an algorithm is partitioned among the machine's available processors. This has the dual disadvantage of being tedious for the programmer and static in nature. Although it may be possible for some programs to be partitioned such that work is distributed reasonably evenly among all processors, static partitioning is limited in what it can do. In general, the amount of work being done by the different processes that comprise the program changes with time. This means that one particular distribution of processes among processors may distribute the workload among those processors rather evenly at one time and quite unevenly at a later time. It would be preferable to have the system recognize when the workload becomes too unbalanced, and redistribute processes to even out that workload, and to have this happen dynamically, as the program is running. The Myrias SPS-3's operating system dynamically and automatically balances workload during execution to keep processors busy by assigning and reassigning tasks to available processors.

Memory and Storage Considerations. The goal of a memory system is to deliver instructions and data to processors at a rate necessary to sustain unhampered performance. If a computer is capable of performing one billion operations per second, the memory system must be able to supply its processing elements with one billion instructions and perhaps two billion data items per second. The perfect memory system is, therefore, an infinitely large storage area with instantaneous response (unfortunately, there are no companies currently delivering such a system). Systems that are on the market today try to mimic the perfect system with a hierarchy of storage devices, each with different characteristics.

In most systems, data and instructions are on disks for long-term storage. Since even the fastest disks keep most supercomputers and parallel computers waiting for data, a software mechanism called *disk striping* is used to increase the transfer rate to and from disk storage. Disk striping stores data on multiple disks and reads and writes data in parallel. With disk striping, data is divided into blocks and distributed across multiple disks—the first block on the first disk, the second block on the second disk, etc.— so that multiple reads and writes can be performed in parallel. If an application program requests more than one numerically contiguous block at a time, it benefits from an increased transfer rate as disk drives transfer data into the system in parallel.

Disk access is usually controlled by specialized I/O processors separate from those processors used to perform the actual computations. This frees the computational processors from having to handle their own I/O requests and allows the I/O processors to be optimized for I/O operations.

Data read from disk is usually written into a semiconductor memory system. The path from I/O subsystem to memory is usually called the main system bus (although, on some multiprocessors, there is no main bus). The rate at which data can be moved over this bus should be sufficient to handle the I/O subsystem's ability to transfer data to and from memory, or else it represents a bottleneck and renders at least part of the I/O subsystem's capability useless. In practice, it may be more difficult to determine whether the bus's transfer rate is sufficient, since the same bus may also carry traffic between processors and memory and other devices. One simple method is to sum the peak rates of the various subsystems and see if the bus can sustain that total transfer rate. This is more complicated than it sounds, however, since there are several mechanisms that can be used to reduce a processor's load on main memory.

One mechanism to reduce the time it takes a processor to access memory and to reduce the contention among memory accesses by different processors is a local *memory cache*. The idea behind memory caching came from the observation that most programs often reuse instruction sequences (for example, in loops) and/or data. If a processor can successfully retrieve the information it needs from a small localized memory (cache), the number of main memory accesses it has to make is reduced. This has two benefits: it reduces contention for both the memory bus and memory, and it allows slower, less costly parts to be used in main memory. Even with a cache, main memory still needs to transfer data at a very high bandwidth to the processor/cache subsystem. To obtain this bandwidth, memory access can be interleaved in the same way as disk files can be striped. By constructing main memory from a number of memory banks, multiple memory accesses can be performed in parallel.

Most caches work on the principle that a programmer does not understand the patterns of execution of a program well enough to specify what should be held in a cache; the hardware simply holds what was used most recently. High-speed caches connected to each processor maintain local copies of memory locations and supply operands and instructions at the rate required by each processor. However, the existence of multiple copies of data gives rise to a *cache-coherency* problem where multiple copies of the same memory location must be kept consistent even while in the different processors' cache [Dubois:90]. Solving the cache coherency problem is an active question being pursued by industry and academia alike.

A system's memory access time is dependent on all the factors above. Once a processor's speed is known, the required speeds for the rest of the system can be calculated. The size of the cache needed to ensure that a sufficient number (more than 90 percent) of memory accesses are cache accesses can also be calculated. The amount of cache, main memory, and disk memory required is application dependent.

Scalability. By scalability, we mean the ability to realize more computing power by adding more processors, memory, or both to a system. A system that could be scaled perfectly would provide double the performance if twice as many processors were furnished. In reality, systems cannot be scaled up arbitrarily. For example, shared-memory machines ultimately run out of bus bandwidth as processors are added. Currently, the machines that offer the greatest scalability are distributed-memory message-passing systems.

In addition to asking how far a particular architecture can be scaled, it may be important to ask how incrementally it can be scaled. For example, in order to increase the size of a hypercube network with 2^N processors, it is necessary to add 2^N processors, taking the system from an N-dimensional cube to an (N+1)-dimensional cube. The need (and the cost) to scale up a system by doubling its size is a constraint of which potential users should be aware. In addition, if the original nodes do not contain enough communications channels for the upgrade, then the nodes will have to be replaced as well.

Software Environment. When reviewing hardware performance specifications for different machines, it is sometimes easy to get lost in the quest for the hottest hardware and to forget that the best hardware is useless without good software-development tools.

The first consideration is language support. All supercomputers mentioned in this report support variations of FORTRAN. Most also support C and many support even LISP. As discussed in section 3, Ada is also becoming more and more available on parallel computers. However, whether a favorite language is available on a particular machine should not be the only consideration in its selection.

The availability of a particular language maybe as important as (if not more important than) the quality of the program development environment that is offered for a machine. An important question is whether a concurrent debugger is available for the language of choice. The additional complexity of expressing concurrency has made debugging parallel programs much harder than debugging sequential programs. When multiple processors are executing in parallel, two situations arise that do not arise in uniprocessor machines. The first situation is that in the presence of an error, repeated executions of the same program using the same input data can produce different results. Two processors may read and write the same memory location in a different order in different runs, thereby producing different results. Secondly, in distributed systems, there may not be a global state and it is, therefore, difficult to determine the exact order of events [McDowell:89].

A debugger assists in locating, analyzing, and correcting suspected errors. Naturally, commercial multiprocessor vendors first provided debuggers that were modifications of their uniprocessor counterparts. These traditional debuggers primarily mimic source-level debuggers, in that the user can step through the program execution one line at a time. Each parallel process can then be examined through its own debugger. There are two main disadvantages to these debuggers. First, with many processors the traditional debugging approach quickly becomes unwieldy; therefore, there is a need to coordinate the debugging results using global commands. Secondly, the debugger is typically intrusive; that is, the debugger may alter the results of the execution, because its use can impact the timing of the interactions of processors and memory.

Researchers are currently investigating several different approaches to improving concurrent debugging. Most of these investigations include the use of windows, graphics, and visualization techniques to provide a higher-level view of program execution [McDowell:89]. Although most of the more advanced, sophisticated, concurrent debuggers are prototypes, there are a few that are commercially available. For example, Intel provides a debugger with the iPSC/860 that allows the user to specify commands on a group of processors. In addition, Encore (under DARPA funding) has developed a non-intrusive parallel debugger called Parasight [Aral:88]. Parasight provides high-level debugging and monitoring capabilities along with low-level profiling tools. Finally, MITRE researchers are combining execution replay with automated analysis to debug parallel programs [Lafferty:90, Hunter:90].

The problem of debugging in a multiprocessor environment is far more than simply a problem of user interface design. Tools for debugging multiprocessor systems are still being developed. This, coupled with the difficulty of writing parallel programs in the first place, may continue to make parallel software development more expensive than sequential software development for some time to come.

In addition, although some vendors provide performance monitoring tools (that is, tools that show how well the application is utilizing the resources of the machine), these tools have widely differing capabilities and are not available on all machines. Finally, developing large software systems for parallel computers is a very complex task. The entire software lifecycle, which includes requirements definition, prototyping, preliminary and detailed design, coding, testing, validation and verification, and maintenance, has to be reviewed, modified, and tailored to address the additional complexity of concurrent computing.

4.3 Comparing Machines

Peak versus Sustained Speed. Claims of peak machine speed by manufacturers are generally true. They are not, however, good indicators of machine performance because few applications can exercise a parallel machine continually at peak speed (MITRE's quadratic-sieve integer-factoring algorithm is an example of one such application that does). It is more typical to obtain perhaps only 25 percent of peak speed on a sustained basis [Hwang:87].

Speedup/Efficiency. The measures of speedup and efficiency provide insight on whether a parallel computer is being effectively utilized for a particular program. Speedup is the ratio of the execution time of the application on one processor to that of the execution time on N processors. Efficiency, in turn, is defined to be the average utilization of the N processors allocated to execute the parallel program.

Attractive as parallel techniques are for attaining ever-increasing computing capability, it is important to understand that all code cannot be run in parallel, and that even if 90 percent of an algorithm or program can be executed in parallel, the 10 percent that must be executed sequentially may in actuality determine how fast the program as a whole can be executed.

Typical applications contain steps, often referred to as the *serial* work, that must be performed before and after the parallel computation takes place. For example, typical steps which must be done sequentially are obtaining parameters, setting up the computation, creating displays, sending and receiving messages between processors, and performing input/output procedures. *Amdahl's Law* is based on fixed-size speedup; that is, the percentage of serial work does not change as the problem size increases.

Researchers at Sandia National Laboratories, however, realized that, in practice, problem size scales with the number of processors; that is, the percentage of serial work changes as the problem size varies.

Sandia's Law is a figure of merit based upon scaled speedup, which better represents speedup for practical problems [Gustafson:88]. Both fixed-size (Amdahl's Law) and scaled (Sandia's Law) speedup depend on different assumptions about the relation between problem size and the number of processors [Denning:88]. Sandia's researchers have been able to attain impressive speedups of over 1,020 on a 1,024 hypercube computer for practical applications. On the other hand, Amdahl's Law predicts a speedup limit of no more than 250. Both laws have to be carefully applied and not blindly used to predict performance.

At MITRE, we have evaluated the performance of a simplified program for calculating target engagement opportunities for a set of weapon platforms against possible deployed missiles. Different parallelization approaches were used to evaluate the performance of the Encore Multimax 320 [Michaud:90b] and the Alliant FX/80 [Michaud:90a].

Benchmarks. While there are many different measures used to compare machines, such as price/performance, speedup, and efficiency [Karp:90], benchmarking is the most effective approach to evaluating the performance of existing machines. Benchmarking is the measurement of specifically defined parameters (for example, execution time, memory use) and their subsequent comparison to known measurements of the same parameters on existing systems. In particular, a hierarchical benchmarking approach is currently the most accepted procedure [Dongarra:87, McCullough:88]. The hierarchical benchmarking approach, although time-consuming, ensures that no essential information is eliminated (e.g., the CPU is fast, but the input/output speeds are intolerably slow). Six levels of programs are benchmarked: basic input/output operations, program kernels, basic routines, stripped-down versions of major applications, full applications, and developmental programs. Be wary of stated manufacturer's claims that program X ran at Y MIPS on their machine, since they often optimize code so that it performs well on their particular machine. They may also compile it on their latest experimental compiler, run it on a specially built machine with slightly faster hardware, and so on. Keep in mind that there is no single machine that out performs all others for all programs. In many cases, the architecture of one machine is a more natural one for a given set of algorithms, because it may better reflect the internal structure of those algorithms.

Manufacturers may also provide the benchmark results for program kernel and basic routines as an indication of their computer's performance. As mentioned above, it must be remembered that the program kernel and basic routines provide only partial information in the benchmarking hierarchy. Nonetheless, the most popular set of program kernels are the Livermore FORTRAN kernels which are representative of the computationally intensive portions of actual programs used at Lawrence Livermore

National Laboratory. This set of program kernels tends to concentrate on simple loops, however, and does not always accurately represent system performance. The most popular basic routines are the LINPACK routines, which are routines that solve a linear system of equations [Dongarra:90]. Finally, The Perfect Benchmarks initiated in 1987 by D. J. Kuck and A. H. Sameh of the University of Illinois are thirteen FORTRAN application programs in various engineering and science fields [Cybenko:90]. The Perfect Benchmark's methodology is applied to all the executions of the application programs on various computers ranging from supercomputers to workstations [Pointer:90].

In summary, it is imperative to remember that there is no universal number that will characterize system performance. The actual performance of a computer is dependent on many factors including architecture, application, language, programmer skill, and workload of the system. However, benchmarks, if properly integrated, can provide insight into the performance of a computer for a specific application.

SECTION 5

SUMMARY AND PERSPECTIVES

This document provides an overview of parallel computing issues and terminology. It describes the more popular, readily available parallel and supercomputer architectures and discusses different language approaches to parallel computation. The actual details of the machines and languages will change with time, but the fundamental issues and basic concerns remain the same. Indeed, efforts to survey the industry quickly reveal that new companies are constantly being formed while others disappear. Nonetheless, the industry as a whole manifests strength, vitality, and excitement, even though parallel computing is still very much in its infancy.

While tremendous computational power is already available through modern super-computers and parallel computer architectures, the technologies being applied to the area of parallel processing are constantly improving. Device speeds are becoming faster, the number of gates per chip is increasing, the power needed per gate is dropping, and the number of pins per chip is increasing. In fact, many experts use the "2 by 2" rule that states that "everything doubles in two years." If this rule continues to apply, we will see great advances in hardware design in the near future. These advances will give rise to both new machine architectures using innovative approaches and more traditional architectures with faster components. Software languages and paradigms are also rapidly evolving. Old and familiar languages are being recast for the parallel computing environment and new paradigms are being created.

One of the greatest concerns of politicians, computer scientists, scientists, and engineers alike, however, is that theoretical breakthroughs in compiler technology, languages, and implementations of practical software environments have not kept pace with the hardware. As Senator Gore remarked at a symposium on supercomputers "... the benefits of supercomputing do not come from the creation of the machines; they come from the use of the machines. And we are not using the machines" [NAS:89]. This problem does not arise from a shortage of computationally intensive problems or for lack of access to supercomputers, because the United States has four National Supercomputer Centers which are constantly upgrading and expanding their computing resources. Instead, the underutilization of supercomputer resources seems to occur for two primary reasons. First, the potential application users do not understand how supercomputers and parallel processing can be used to more effectively solve their problems. Secondly, researchers who are using high-performance computers are frequently failing to take full advantage of the machine. For example, some researchers who have access to a four-processor Cray still use the Cray as a uniprocessor machine.

The first part of the underutilization problem can be solved by better education and communication between researchers. If one scientist or engineer sees or hears of colleagues making great strides using a high-performance computer, that individual may be more willing to extend his research to include the use of supercomputers or parallel machines. The second part of the problem will be solved by better compilers with enhanced capabilities for more automatic vectorization and concurrentization, by languages that are portable between machines, by improved software development tools so that the application user does not have to be a computer scientist, and by visualization.

Visualization is an important new research area that allows huge quantities of result data to be displayed visually. Since supercomputers and parallel machines normally generate large amounts of data, visualization and animation provide three-dimensional color ·images of a scientific process or object that more clearly depict essential relationships in complex n-dimensional models.

To facilitate greater access to modern supercomputers and parallel machines, the National Science Foundation (NSF) has developed a national computer network, NSFNET. This backbone network "... is used to access resources such as supercomputers, libraries, and satellite data, as well as to link geographically dispersed researchers, educators, and scholars" [Forefronts:90]. Regional networks connect major university networks to the backbone NSFNET. After its current expansion is completed, NSFNET will be the "world's fastest openly available network for research and education ..." [Forefronts:90]. In addition, NSF and DARPA are providing funds for five gigabit test beds to explore the prospects for gigabit networks in order to support, for example, transferring of visual images [Turner:90].

In the future, we can expect to see massively parallel teraflop machines. These machines will be supported by gigabit networks which will allow grand-challenge problems to be solved by using several supercomputers and parallel machines concurrently. In addition, the user network interface will be transparent; that is, the user will not have to perform incredible gyrations to access machines, transfer files, and see the results. The user will not even have to be aware that different machines are being accessed. Finally, many of the grand-challenge problems require very large databases that may be accessed intuitively rather than by the more traditional relational access. Ideally, different users will be able to access the same databases by the access method convenient for their specific computational requirements.

LIST OF REFERENCES

[Ackerman:82] Ackerman, W. B., "Data Flow Languages," *Computer*, Vol. 15, No. 2, February 1982.

[Ada IC:90a] *Ada Information Clearing House Newsletter*, Ada Information Clearing House, Vol. VIII, No. 2, June 1990.

[Ada IC:90b] *Ada Validated Compiler List*, Ada Information Clearing House, Washington, DC, 1 May 1990.

[Agha:86] Agha, G. A., *ACTORS: A Model of Concurrent Computation in Distributed Systems*, Cambridge, MA: MIT Press, 1986.

[Ahmed:91] Ahmed, S., and N. Cariero, and D. Gelernter, "The Linda Program Builder", *Advances in Languages and Compilers for Parallel Processing*, A. Nicolau, D. Gelernter, T. Gross, and D. Padua (editors), Cambridge, MA: MIT Press, 1991.

[Alliant:88a] *FX/Fortran Language Manual*, Alliant Computer Systems Corporation, Littleton, MA, July 1988.

[Alliant:88b] *FX/Fortran Programmer's Handbook*, Alliant Computer Systems Corporation, Littleton, MA, July 1988

[Andrews:83] Andrews, G. R., and F. B. Schneider, "Concepts and Notations for Concurrent Programming," *ACM Computing Surveys*, Vol. 15, No. 1, March 1983.

[Aral:88] Aral, Z., and I. Gertner, *Parasight: A High-Level Debugger/Profiler Architecture for Shared-Memory Multiprocessors*, ETR 88-005, Encore Computer Corporation, 1988.

[Arvind:90] Arvind and R. S. Nikhil, "Executing a Program on the MIT Tagged-Token Data Flow Architecture," *IEEE Transactions on Computers*, Vol. 39, No. 3, March 1990.

[Athas:89] Athas, W. C., Boden, N.J., "Cantor: An Actor Programming System for Scientific Computing", *Proceedings of the ACM Sigplan Workshop on Object-Based Concurrent Programming*, Sigplan Notices, Vol. 24, No. 4, April 1989.

[Barry:89] Barry, B. M., "Prototyping Real-Time Embedded System in Smalltalk," *Proceedings of the OOPSLA '89, Conference on Object-Oriented Programming Systems, Languages, and Applications*, New Orleans, LA, October 1989.

[Barry:87] Barry, B. M., D. A. Thomas, "Using Objects to Design and Build Radar ESM Systems," *Proceedings of the OOPSLA '87, Conference on Object Oriented Programming Systems, Languages, and Applications*, Orlando, FL, October 1987.

[Bell:89] Bell, G., "The Future of High Performance Computers in Science and Engineering," *Communications of the ACM*, Vol. 32, No. 9, September 1989.

[Bensley:89] E. H. Bensley, T. J. Brando, J. C. Fohlin, M. J. Prelle, A. M. Wollrath, *MITRE's Future Generation Computer Architecture Program*, SIGPLAN, April 1989.

[Bensley:88a] Bensley, E. H., T. J. Brando, E. L. Lafferty, M. J. Prelle, R. D. Silverman, and S. J. Stuart, *Introduction to Parallel Supercomputing*, M88-42, The MITRE Corporation, Bedford, MA, October 1988.

[Bensley:88b] E. H. Bensley, T. J. Brando, M. J. Prelle, "An Execution Model for Distributed Object-Oriented Computation," *Proceedings of the OOPSLA '88 (Object-Oriented Programming Systems, Languages and Architectures) Conference*, September, 1988.

[Burton:88] Burton, F. W., and J. G. Kollias, "Functional Programming with Quadtrees," *IEEE Software*, Vol. 5, No. 1, January 1988.

[Cann:91] Cann, D., "Retire Fortran? A Debate Rekindled", Proceedings of the IEEE sponsored Supercomputing 1991, Albuquerque, NM, November, 1991.

[Carriero:89] Carriero, N., and D. Gelernter, "Linda in Context," *Communications of the ACM*, Vol. 32, No. 4, April 1989.

[Cenkl:91] Cenkl, M. and C.L. Nowacki, "Techniques for Mapping Algorithms to Parallel Signal Processors," MTR-11266, The MITRE Corporation, Bedford, MA, to be released.

[Cleary:89] Cleary, J., *Experience with Sim++: The Jade Distributed Discrete Event Simulation System*, Jade Simulations International Corporation, 1989.

[Cox:86] Cox, B. J., *Object-Oriented Programming: An Evolutionary Approach*, Reading MA: Addison-Wesley, 1986.

[Cybenko:90] Cybenko, G., L. Kipp, L. Pointer, and D. Kuck, *Supercomputer Performance Evaluation and the Perfect Benchmarks*, University of Illinois, CSRD Report No. 965, March 1990.

[Dally:89] Dally, W. J., A. A. Chien, *"Object-Oriented Concurrent Programming in CST,"* *Proceedings of the ACM Sigplan Workshop on Object-Based Concurrent Programming, Sigplan Notices*, Vol. 24, No. 4, April 1989.

[Dally:87] Dally, W. J., and C. L. Seitz, "Deadlock-Free Message Routing in Multiprocessor Interconnection Networks," *IEEE Transactions on Computers*, Vol. C-36, No. 5, May 1987.

[Davidson:89] Davidson, C., Technical Correspondence, *Communications of the ACM*, Vol. 32, No. 10, October 1989.

[Denning:88] Denning, P. J., "Speeding Up Parallel Processing," *American Scientist*, Vol. 76, July/August 1988.

[DOD:83] *Reference Manual for the Ada Programming Language*, ANSI/MIL-STD-1815A, U.S. Department of Defense, 17 February 1983.

[Dongarra:90] Dongarra, J. J., *Performance of Various Computers Using Standard Linear Equations Software*, CS89-85, University of Tennessee, 17 August 1990.

[Dongarra:87] Dongarra, J., J. L. Martin, and J. Worlton, *Evaluating Computers and their Performance: Perspectives, Pitfalls, and Paths*, RC1294 (#57657), IBM Research Center, June 1987.

[DSB:87] *Report of the Defense Science Board Task Force on Military Software*, Defense Science Board, September 1987.

[Dubois:90] Dubois, M., and S. Thakkar, "Cache Architectures in Tightly Coupled Multiprocessors," *Computer*, Vol. 23, No. 6, June 1990.

[Forefronts:90] "NSFNET to Undergo Expansion," *Forefronts*, Cornell University, Vol. 6, No. 3, July/August 1990.

[Garfinkel:91] Garfinkel, S., and G. Spafford, *Practical UNIX Security*, O'Reilly and Associates, Inc., Sebastopol, CA, 1991.

[Gelernter:88] Gelernter, D., "Getting the Job Done," *BYTE*, Vol. 13, No. 11, November 1988.

[Gill:90] McCreary, C. L., and D. H. Gill, "Efficient Exploitation of Concurrency Using Graph Decomposition," *Proceedings of the 1990 International Conference on Parallel Processing, Vol. 2*, August 1990.

[Gill:89] McCreary, C. L., and D. H. Gill, "Automatic Determination of Grain Size for Efficient Parallel Processing," *Communications of the ACM*, Vol. 32, No. 9, September 1989,.pp. 1073-1078.

[Goldberg:83] Goldberg, A., Smalltalk-80: The Language and Implementation, Reading, MA: Addison-Wesley, 1983.

[Gustafson:88] Gustafson, J. L., "Re-evaluating Amdahl's Law," *Communications of the ACM*, Vol. 31, No. 5, May 1988.

[Herbst:91] Herbst,K., "Motorola/MIT Monsoon is First U.S. Dataflow Prototype," *Supercomputing Review*, Vol. 4, No. 11, November 1991.

[Hoare:78] Hoare, C. A. R., "Communicating Sequential Processes," *CACM* 21:8, 1978.

[Hockney: 88] Hockney, R. W. and C. R. Jesshope, Parallel Computers 2, Philadelphia, PA: Adam Hilger, 1988.

[Hudak:89] Hudak, P., "Conception, Evolution, and Application of Functional Programming Languages," *ACM Computing Survey*, Vol. 21, No. 3, September 1989.

[Hunter:91] Hunter, C. D., "An Integrated Approach to Replay Analysis of Message-Passing Parallel Programs" Proceedings of the IEEE sponsored Supercomputing Debugging Workshop, Albuquerque, NM, November 1991.

[Hunter:90] Hunter, C. D., *Debugging Highly Parallel Programs: Toward Fundamental Techniques*, MTR 11046, The MITRE Corporation, Bedford, MA, December 1990

[Hwang:85] Hwang, K., "Multiprocessor Supercomputers for Scientific/Engineering Applications," *Computer*, Vol. 18, No. 6, June 1985.

[Hwang:87] Hwang, K., "Advanced Parallel Processing with Supercomputers Architectures," *Proceedings of the IEEE*, Vol. 75, No. 10, October 1987.

[Hwang:84] Hwang, K., and F. A. Briggs, *Computer Architecture and Parallel Processing*, New York, NY: McGraw-Hill, Inc., 1984.

[SSS: 89] IEEE Scientific Supercomputer Subcommittee, "Supercomputing: Supercomputer Hardware," *Computer*, Vol. 22, No.11, November 1989.

[Intel:89] "iPSC/2 Concurrent Programming Workshop," *Intel Scientific Computers*, 1989.

[Jagannathan:89] Jagannathan, S., *A Programming Language Supporting First-Class Parallel Environments*, MIT/LCS/TR-434, Massachusetts Institute of Technology, January 1989.

[Jamieson:87] Jamieson, L. H., D. B. Gannon, and R. J. Douglas, *The Characteristics of Parallel Algorithms*, Cambridge, MA: The MIT Press, 1987.

[Jefferson:87] Jefferson, D., et al., "Distributed Simulation and the Time Warp Operating System," *Proceedings Eleventh ACM Symposium on Operating Systems Principles*, Austin, TX, November 1987.

[Karp:90] Karp, A. H., and H. P. Flatt, "Measuring Parallel Processor Performance," *Communications of the ACM*, Vol. 33, No. 5, May 1990.

[Keene:88] Keene, S. E., *Object-Oriented Programming in Common Lisp*, Reading, MA: Addison-Wesley, 1988.

[Kreutzer:86] Kreutzer, W., *System Simulation Programming Styles and Languages*, Reading, MA: Addison-Wesley, 1986.

[Lafferty:90] Lafferty, E. L., and C. D. Hunter,*Parallel Computing FY90 Final Report*, MTR 10985, The MITRE Corporation, Bedford,MA, October 1990.

[Lippman:89] Lippman, S. B., *C++ Primer*, Reading, MA: Addison-Wesley, 1989.

[McCullough:88] McCullough, B., "Parallel Processing Systems Demand Tailored Benchmarks," *Computer Design*, November 1988.

[McDowell:89] McDowell, C. E., and D. P. Helmbold, "Debugging Concurrent Programs," *ACM Computing Surveys*, Vol. 21, No. 4, December 1989.

[Meyer:88] Meyer, B., *Object-Oriented Software Construction*, Englwood Cliffs, NJ: Prentice-Hall, 1988.

[Michaud:91] Michaud, M. C., G. M. Whittaker, J. B. Goethert, and M. A. Schroeder, "Parallelism in Signal Processing Algorithms: Final Report," MTR 10824, The MITRE Corporation, Bedford, MA, October 1991

[Michaud:90a] Michaud, M. C., and J. B. Goethert, *An Evaluation of Processing Efficiency on Multi-Processor Architectures, Vol. 2: Alliant FX/80*, MTR 9291, The MITRE Corporation, Bedford, MA, May 1990.

[Michaud:90b] Michaud, M. C., M. A. Schroeder, and J. B. Goethert, *An Evaluation of Processing Efficiency on Multi-Processor Architectures, Vol. 1: Encore Multimax*, MTR 9291, The MITRE Corporation, Bedford, MA, January 1990.

[NAS:89] "Supercomputers - Directions in Technology and Applications," *National Academy of Sciences*, Washington DC: National Academy Press, 1989.

[Nelson:90] Nelson, V. P., "Fault-Tolerant Computing: Fundamental Concepts," *Computer*, Vol. 23, No..7, July 1990.

[Nowacki:92] Nowacki, C. L., "An Uninterpreted Simulation Model of a Cluster Array Processor," chapter 3 in *Performance and Fault Modeling* in VHDL, J.M. Schoen, ed., (NY:Prentice-Hall) 1992.

[Pointer:90] Pointer, L., *Perfect: Performance Evaluation for Cost-Effective Transformations Report 2*, CSRD Report. No. 964, University of Illinois, March 1990.

[Prelle:92] Prelle, M. J. and A. M. Wollrath, *The SaM Synchronization Manager Distributed Object-Oriented Programming FY91 Final Report*, MTR 11229, The MITRE Corporation, Bedford, MA, January, 1992.

[Prelle:91] Prelle, M. J., A. M. Wollrath, T. J. Brando, E. H. Bensley, *The Impact of Selected Concurrent Language Constructs on the SaM Runtime System*, OOPS Messenger, ACM Press, Vol. 2, No. 2, April, 1991.

[Prelle:90] Prelle, M. J., T. J. Brando, E. H. Bensley, J. I. Leivent, R. J. Watro, A. M. Wollrath, *Distributed Object-Oriented Programming FY90 Final Report*, MTR 11058, The MITRE Corporation, Bedford, MA, December, 1990.

[Royce:90] Royce, W., "Reusable Ada Components for Large, Distributed Multi-task Networks: NAS," *Defense Science*, Vol. 9, No. 1, January 1990.

[Royce:89] Royce, W., "Reliable, Reusable Ada Components for Constructing Large, Distributed Multi-Task Networks: Network Architecture Series (NAS)," *Proceedings of TriAda '89*, 1989.

[Sawchuk:87] Sawchuk, A. A., B. K. Jenkins, C. S. Raghavendra, and A. Varma,"Optical Crossbar Networks," *Computer*, Vol. 20, No. 6, June 1987.

[Siewiorek:90] Siewiorek, D. P., "Fault Tolerance in Commercial Computers," *Computer*. Vol. 23, No. 7, July 1990.

[SigAda:89] "Approved Ada Language Commentaries," *Ada Letters*, Vol. 9, No. 3, Spring 1989.

[Silverman:91] Silverman, R. D., "Massively Distributed Computing and Factoring Large Integers,"*Communications of the ACM*, Vol. 34, No. 11, November 1991

[Silverman:90] Silverman, R. D., "Parallel Polynomial Multiplication over Finite Rings," J. Parallel and Distributed Computing, Vol. 10, pp. 265-270, 1990.

[Silverman:89] Stuart, S. J. and R. D. Silverman, "A Distributed Batching System for Parallel Processing," *Software Practice and Experience*, Vol. 19, pp. 1163-1174, 1989.

[Silverman:88] Caron, T. R. and R. D. Silverman, "Parallel Implementation of the Quadratic Sieve," *The Journal of Supercomputing*, Vol. 1, No. 3, pp. 273-290, 1988.

[Smotroff:90] Smotroff, I. G., *Dataflow Architectures: Flexible Platforms for Neural Network Simulation*, M90-10, The MITRE Corporation, Bedford, MA, January 1990.

[Sokol:89] Sokol, L. M., B. K. Stucky and V. Whang, "MTW: A Control Mechanism for Parallel Discrete Simulation," *Proceedings of the International Conference on Parallel Processing, IEEE Computer Society*, 1989.

[Stroustrup:87] Stroustrup, B., *The C++ Programming Language*, Reading, MA: Addison-Wesley, 1987.

[Turner:90] Turner, J. A., "Washington to Upgrade NSFNET, Prepare for Gigabit Network," *Supercomputing Review*, Vol. 13, No. 8, August 1990.

[Uhr:87] Uhr, L., *Multi-Computer Architectures for Artificial Intelligence*, New York, NY: John Wiley & Sons, 1987.

[Wegner:80] Wegner, P., *Programming with Ada*, Englewood Cliffs, NJ: Prentice-Hall, Inc., 1980.

[Whiddett:87] Whiddett, D., *Concurrent Programming for Software Engineers*, New York, NY: Wiley and Sons, 1987.

[Yonezawa:87] Yonezawa, A., E. Shibayama, T. Takada, and Y. Honda, *Modeling and Programming in Object-Oriented Concurrent Language ABCL/1*, in "Object-Oriented Concurrent Programming,' edited by A. Yonezawa and M. Tokoro, Cambridge, MA: MIT Press, 1987.

BIBLIOGRAPHY

A Catalog of Interface Features and Options for the Ada Run Time Environment, Ada Run Time Environment Working Group Interface Subgroup, Release 1.0, October 1986.

Agerwala, T., and Arvind, "Data Flow Systems," *Computer*, Vol. 15, No. 2, February 1982.

Ahuja, S., N. Carriero, D. Gelernter, and V. Krishnaswamy, "Matching Language and Hardware for Parallel Computation in the Linda Machine," *IEEE Transactions on Computers*, Vol. 37, No. 8, August 1988.

Ahuja, S., N. Carriero, and D. Gelernter, "Linda and Friends," *Computer*, Vol. 19, No. 8, August 1988.

Air Force Policy on Programming Languages, Department of the Air Force (letter), 9 November 1988.

Air Force Programming Language Policy Clarification, Department of the Air Force (letter), 7 December 1989.

"A Model Run Time System Interface for Ada, Version 2.3," Ada Run Time Environment Working Group MRTSI Task Force, *Ada Letters*, Vol. IX, No. 1, January/February 1989.

Andrews, G. R., and F. B. Schneider, "Concepts and Notations for Concurrent Programming," *ACM Computer Surveys*, Vol. 15, No. 1, March 1983.

Arvind, and R. S. Nikhil, *A Dataflow Approach to General-Purpose Parallel Computing*, CSG 302, Massachusetts Institution of Technology, Cambridge, MA, 7 July 1989.

Babb, R. G., *Programming Parallel Processors*, Reading, MA: Addison-Wesley, 1988.

Bal, H. E., J. G. Steiner, and A. S. Tanenbaum, "Programming Languages for Distributed Computing Systems," *ACM Computing Surveys*, Vol. 21, No. 3, September 1989.

Bamberger, J., et al., *Kernel Facilities Definition*, working paper version 2.0, 15 April 1988.

Bjornson, R., N. Carriero, and D. Gelernter, *The Implementation and Performance of Hypercube Linda*, RR-690, Yale University, March 1989.

Bjornson, R., N. Carriero, D. Gelernter, and J. S. Leichter, *Linda the Portable Parallel*, Research Report YALE/DCS/RR-520, Yale University, January 1988.

Booch, G., *Software Engineering with Ada*, Reading, MA: Benjamin/Cummings Publishing Company, 1987.

Borger, M. W., M. H. Klein, and R. A. Veltre, *Real-Time Software Engineering in Ada: Observations and Guidelines*, Technical Report CMU/SEI-89-TR-22, Software Engineering Institute at Carnegie-Mellon University, September 1989.

Brando, T. J., H. E. T. Connell, J. D. Harris, M. J. Prelle, "A Massively Parallel Artificial Intelligence Processor," *Proceedings of the Fifth Annual International Phoenix Conference on Computers and Communications*, Scottsdale, AZ, March 1986.

Brooks, E. D. III, *Effective Use of Shared Memory Multiprocessors*, DE88-007019, Lawrence Livermore National Laboratory, February 1988.

Browne, J. C., M. Azam, and S. Sobek, "CODE: A Unified Approach to Parallel Programming," *IEEE Software*, Vol. 6, No. 4, July 1989.

Buhr, R. J. A., *System Design with Ada*, Englewood Cliffs, NJ: Prentice-Hall, 1984.

Carriero, N., *Implementing Tuple Space Machines*, Doctoral Dissertation, Yale University, 1987.

Carriero, N., and D. Gelernter, "How to Write Parallel Programs: A Guide to the Perplexed," *ACM Computing Surveys*, Vol. 21, No. 3, September 1989.

Carriero, N., and D. Gelernter, *Coordination Languages and Their Significance*, Research Report, Yale University, June 1989.

Carriero, N., and D. Gelernter, "Applications Experience with Linda," *ACM/SIGPLAN PPEALS, SIGPLAN NOTICES*, Vol. 23, No. 9, September 1988.

Carriero, N., and D. Gelernter, "The S/Net's Linda Kernel," *ACM Transactions* on *Computer Systems*, May 1986.

Carriero. N., D. Gelernter, and J. S. Leichter, "Distributed Data Structures in Linda," *Proceedings of the ACM*, Symposium on Principles of Programming Languages, January 1986.

Center, J., *Developing Software to Use Parallel Processing Effectively*, RADC-TR-88-203, October 1988.

Chandy, K. M., and J. Misra, *Parallel Program Design*, Reading, MA: Addison-Wesley, 1988.

Connell, H. E. T., and J. D. Harris, *An Interconnection Scheme for a Tightly Coupled Massively Parallel Computer Network*, International Conference on Computer Design: VLSI in Computers, Port Chester, NY, October 1985.

Cornhill, D., "A Survivable Distributed Computing System for Embedded Application Programs Written in Ada," *Ada Letters*, Vol. 4, No. 4, November 1987.

Cornhill, D., and L. Sha, "Priority Inversion in Ada," *Ada Letters*, Vol. 7, No. 7, November 1987.

Cornhill, D., L. Sha, J. P. Lehoczky, R. Rajkumar, and H. Tokuda, "Limitations of Ada for Real-Time Scheduling," *Proceeding of the International Workshop Real-Time Ada Issues*, November 1987.

Davis, A. L., and R. M. Keller, "Data Flow Program Graphs," *Computer*, Vol. 15, No. 2, February 1982.

Duncan, R., A Survey of Parallel Computer Architectures, *Computer*, Vol. 23, No. 2, February 1990.

Eisenbach, S., "Functional Programming: Languages, Tools and Architectures," *Ellis Horwood Books*, New York: John Wiley & Sons, Inc., 1987.

Ellis, J. R., *Bulldog: A Compiler for VLIW Architectures*, Cambridge, MA: The MIT Press, 1986.

Falk, H., "Revisions and Additions Thrust Ada into Real Time," *Computer Design*, 15 November 1988.

Flaig, C. M., *VLSI Mesh Routing Systems*, M.S. Thesis, Technical Report 5241:TR:87, California Institute of Technology, 1987.

Foster, R., and D. Wilson, "Parallel Programming without Tears III: Architectural Support for Large Applications," *Proceedings of Supercomputing Symposium '88*, June 1988.

Gajski, D. D., D. A. Padua, D. J. Kuck, and R. H. Kuhn, "A Second Opinion in Data Flow Machines and Languages," *Computer*, Vol. 15, No. 2, February 1982.

Ganapathi, M., and G. O. Mendal, "Issues in Ada Compiler Technology," *Computer*, Vol. 22, No. 2, February 1989.

Gelernter, D., "Multiple Tuple Spaces in Linda," *Proceedings Parallel Architectures and Languages Europe (Parle 89)*, Springer-Verlag LNCS 366, Vol. 2, June 1989.

Gelernter, D., "Domesticating Parallelism," *Computer*, Vol. 19, No. 8, August 1986.

Harris, J.D., "Performance Measurements of Parallel Digital Signal Processor Systems," MTR-11263, The MITRE Corporation, Bedford, MA, to be released.

Henson, M. C., *Elements of Functional Languages*, Boston, MA: Blackwell Scientific Publications, 1987.

Hicks, J. E., Jr., *A High-Level Signal Processing Programming Language*, MIT/LCS/TR-414, Massachusetts Institute of Technology, March 1988.

Hillis, W. D., *The Connection Machine*, Cambridge, MA: The MIT Press, 1985.

Horn, B. K. P., *Robot Vision*, New York, NY: McGraw-Hill, 1986.

Hughes, J., "Why Functional Programming Matters," *The Computer Journal*, Vol. 32, No. 2, 1989.

Jefferson, D., et al., "Distributed Simulation and the Time Warp Operating System," *Proceedings of the Eleventh ACM Symposium on Operating Systems Principles*, Austin, TX, November 1987.

Jefferson, D., "Virtual Time," *ACM Transactions on Programming Languages and Systems*, Vol. 7, No. 3, July 1985.

Jefferson, D., and H. Sowizral, *Fast Concurrent Simulation Using the Time Warp Mechanism, Part I: Local Control*, Rand Note N-1906AF, The Rand Corporation, Santa Monica, CA, December 1982.

Jha, R., G. Eisenhower, M. Kamrad, and D. Cornhill, "An Implementation Supporting Distributed Execution of Partitioned Ada Programs," *Ada Letters*, Vol. 9, No. 1, January/February 1989.

Kahn, K. M., and M. S. Miller, Technical Correspondence, *Communications of the ACM*, Vol. 32, No. 10, October 1989.

Kallstrom, and S. S. Thakkar, "Programming Three Parallel Computers," *IEEE Software*, Vol. 5, No. 1, January 1988.

Kamrad, M., R. Jha, G. Eisenhower, and D. Cornhill, "Distributed Ada," *Ada Letters*, Vol. 7, No. 6, May 1987.

Karp, A. H., and R. G. Babb, II, "A Comparison of 12 Parallel FORTRAN Dialects," *IEEE Software*, Vol. 5, No. 5, September 1988.

Karp, A. H., "Programming for Parallelism," *Computer*, Vol. 20, No. 5, May 1987.

Kernel Linda Specification, Technical Note 89.16, Cogent Research, Inc., 1989.

Knuth, D. E., *The Art of Computer Programming, Vol. 2: Seminumerical Algorithms, Second Edition*, Reading, MA: Addison-Wesley, 1981.

Krishnawamy, V., "The Architecture of a Linda Coprocessor," *Proceedings of the ACM Conference on Computer Architectures*, 1988.

Kuhn, R. H., and D. A. Padua, *Tutorial on Parallel Processing*, Silver Spring, MD: IEEE Computer Society Press, 1981.

Lee, C. C., S. Skedzielewski, and J. Feo, "On the Implementation of Applicative Languages on Shared-Memory, MIMD Multiprocessors," *Proceedings of the ACM/SIGPLAN PPEALS, SIGPLAN NOTICES*, Vol. 23, No. 9, September 1988.

Leler, W., "Linda Meets Unix," *Computer*, February 1990.

Lemanski, W. J., *Parallel Ada Implementations of a Multiple Model Kalman Filter Tracking System: A Software Engineering Approach*, DTIC AD-A206 094, March 1989.

Levine, G., "Controlling Anomalies of Concurrent Programming with Ada," *Journal of Pascal, Ada & Modula-2*, Vol. 8, No. 5, September/October 1989.

Lumpp, J. E., Jr., S. A. Fineberg, W. G. Nation, T. L. Casavant, E. C. Bronson, H. J. Siegel, P. H. Pero, T. Schwederski, and D. C. Marinescu, "CAPS: A Coding Aid for PASM," *Communications of the ACM*, Vol.34, No. 11, November 1991

Lundberg, L., "A Parallel Ada System on an Experimental Multiprocessor,"*Software - Practice and Experience*, Vol. 19(8), August 1989.

Matsuoka, S., and S. Kawai, "Using Tuple Space Communication in Distributed Object-Oriented Languages," *OOPSLA '88 Proceedings*, September 1988.

McGrogan, S. R. Olson, and N. Toda, "Parallelizing Large Existing Programs-Methodology and Experiences," *COMPCON '86*, 1986.

McJones, P. R., and G. F. Swart, *Evolving the UNIX System Interface to Support Multithreaded Programs*, Digital Equipment Corporation Systems Research Center, 28 September 1987.

Miller, S. E., *A Survey of Parallel Computing*, RADC-TR-88-129, July 1988.

Misra, J., "Distributed Discrete-Event Simulation," *ACM Computing Surveys*, Vol. 18, No. 1, March 1986.

Mundie, D. A., and D. A. Fisher, "Parallel Processing in Ada," *Computer*, Vol. 19, No. 8, August 1986.

Myers, W., ed., "News Interview with R. Ewald, Vice President of Software, Cray Research, Cray Looks Ahead to Parallel Environments," *IEEE Software*, Vol. 5, No. 1, January 1988.

Myers, W., "Ada: First Users - Pleased; Prospective Users - Still Hesitant," *Computer*, Vol. 20, No. 3, March 1987.

Nielsen, K., and K. Shumate, *Designing Large Real-Time Systems with Ada*, New York, NY: McGraw-Hill, 1988.

Nikhil, R. S., and Arvind, *Programming in Id: a Parallel Programming Language*, The Massachusetts Institute of Technology, 1989.

Nowacki, C. L., J. D. Harris, and M. N. Richard, "Adaptive Beamforming in Quadratic Residue Number Systems on a Cluster Array Processor," in Proc. 1989 IEEE Military Communications Conference (MILCOM), pp. 624-8, October 1989.

Nussbaum, D. and A. Agarwal, "Scalability of Parallel Machines," *Communications of the ACM*, Vol. 34, No. 3, March 1991.

Oldehoeft, R. R., Parallel Functional Computation, ARD 23221.18.EL, 9 November 1989.

Onanian, J. S., A Signal Processing Language for Coarse Grain Dataflow Multiprocessors, MIT/LCS/TR-449, Massachusetts Institute of Technology, 14 June 1989.

Pancake, C. M., and D. Bergmark, December 1990, "Do Parallel Languages Respond to the Needs of Scientific Programmers?," *Computer*, Vol. 23, No. 12.

Pancake, C. M. "Software Support for Parallel Computing: Where Are We Headed?," *Communications of the ACM*, Vol. 34, No. 11, November 1991

Patton, P. C., "Multiprocessors: Architecture and Applications," *Computer*, Vol. 18, No. 6, 1985.

Perrott, R. H., *Parallel Programming*, Reading, MA: Addison-Wesley, 1987.

Perrott, R. H., and A. Zarea-Aliabadi, "Supercomputer Languages," *ACM Computing Surveys*, Vol. 18, No. 1, March 1986.

Peyton Jones, S. L., *The Implementation of Functional Programming Languages*, Prentice-Hall Inc., 1989.

Polychronopoulos, C., *Automatic Restructuring of FORTRAN Programs or Parallel Execution*, CSRD Rpt. No. 665, Center for Supercomputing Research and Development, University of Illinois, May 1987.

Potter, J. L., *The Massively Parallel Processor*, Cambridge, MA: The MIT Press, 1985.

Ramsdell, J. D., "The Alonzo Functional Programming Language," SIGPLAN Notices, Vol. 24, No.9, pp. 152-157, September 1989.

Raveche, H. H., D. H. Laurie, and A. M. Despaim, *A National Computing Initiative - The Agenda for Leadership*, Society for Industrial and Applied Mathematics, Philadelphia, PA, 1987.

Rowe, J., "Producing with Ada - Real-Time Solutions for Complex Problem," *Defense Electronics*, Vol. 22, No. 7, July 1990.

Russell, C. H., and P. J. Waterman, "Variations on UNIX for Parallel Processing Computers," *Communication of the ACM*, Vol. 30, No. 12, December 1987.

Sammet, J. E., "Why Ada is not Just Another Programming Language," *Communication of the ACM*, Vol. 29, No. 8, August 1986.

Sawchuk, A. A., B. K. Jenkins, C. S. Raghavendra, and A. Varma, "Optical Crossbar Networks," *Computer*, Vol. 19, No. 8, August 1986.

Sha, L., and J. B. Goodenough, "Real-Time Scheduling Theory and Ada," *Computer*, Vol. 23, No. 4, April 1990.

Sha, L., J. P. Lehoczky, and R. Rajkumar, "Solutions for Some Practical Problems in Prioritized Preemptive Scheduling," *IEEE Real-Time Systems Symposium*, August 1986.

Shatz, S. M., and J. Wang, "Introduction to Distributed Software Engineering," *Computer*, Vol. 20, No. 10, October 1987.

Shumate, K., *Understanding Concurrency in Ada*, New York: McGraw-Hill, 1988.

Sokol, L. M. and B. K. Stucky, "Improving C^2 Simulation Speed with Parallel Computers," *Proceedings of the 25th Annual Symposium of the Washington Operations Research/Management Science Council*, October 1988; also published in Proceedings of the DCA/JDSSC Computer-Based Modeling of Defense/Offense Issues Symposium, September 1988.

Sokol, L. M., A. P. Wieland and D. P. Briscoe, "MTW: A Strategy for Scheduling Discrete Simulation Messages for Concurrent Execution," *Proceedings of the Distributed Simulation Conference, Society for Computer Simulation*, February 1988.

Sokol, L. M., A. P. Wieland and D. P. Briscoe, "A Time Window Solution to Scheduling Simulation Messages on Parallel Processors," *Proceedings of the Expert Systems in Government Symposium*, IEEE, October 1987.

Stanfill, C., and B. Kahle, "Parallel Free-Text Search on the Connection Machine System," *Communications of the ACM*, Vol. 29, No. 12, December 1986.

Stone, H. S., *High-Performance Computer Architecture*, New York, NY: Addison-Wesley, 1987.

Stone, H. S., "Parallel Querying of Large Databases: A Case Study," *Computer*, Vol. 20, No. 10, 1987.

Tanenbaum, A. S., and R. van Renesse, "Distributed Operating Systems," *ACM Computing Surveys*, Vol. 17, No. 4, December 1985.

Computer Programming Language Policy, DOD Directive 3405.1, U.S. Department of Defense, 2 April 1987.

Use of Ada in Weapon Systems, DOD Directive 3405.2, U.S. Department of Defense, 30 March 1987.

Veen, A. H., "Data Flow Machine Architecture," *ACM Computing Surveys*, Vol. 18, No. 4, December 1986.

Vegdahl, S. R., "A Survey of Proposed Architectures for the Execution of Functional Languages," *IEEE Transactions on Computers*, Vol. C-33, No. 12, pp. 1050-1071, December 1984.

Wallach, S., "Supers Built to Fit," *UNIX Review*, Vol. 8, No. 4, April 1990.

Wallach, Y., *Parallel Processing and Ada*, Englewood Cliffs, NJ: Prentice Hall, 1991.

Whiteside, R. A., and J. S. Leichter, "Using Linda for Supercomputing on a Local Area Network," *Proceedings of Supercomputing '88, BYTE*, November 1988.

Weicker, R. P., December 1990, "An Overview of Common Benchmarks," Computer, Vol. 23, No. 12.

Wilkes, M. V., "The Bandwidth Famine," *Communications of the ACM*, Vol. 33, No. 8, August 1990.

Wolfe, M., "Multiprocessor Synchronization for Concurrent Loops," *IEEE Software*, Vol. 5, No. 1, January 1988.

APPENDIX A

DESCRIPTIONS OF INDIVIDUAL MACHINES

This section contains brief descriptions of most of the machines mentioned in this document, as well as other comparable machines. All these machines are commercially marketed at this time and the information is the most currently available, having been updated in the November-December 1991 time frame. Information on software and available network services has also been included in these descriptions since this is increasingly important to the consumer. However, information that was not applicable and/or available has been omitted from these descriptions. Every attempt has been made to confirm the information being published. All products are trademarks of their respective companies. A summary of the major characteristics of the machines described in this appendix are shown in table A-1.

Alliant FX/2800

System Type
MIMD

Topology
Shared-memory, bus-based

Processor Type
Intel i860

Cycle Time/Clock Rate
25 nsec (40 MHz)

Peak Speed
1.1 GFLOPS double precision (fully
configured with 28 processors)

Number of Processors
4 - 28

Processor Cache
Up to 8 caches of 2 MBYTES each
(16 MBYTES), shared by processors

Processor-to-Cache Bandwidth
1.28 GBYTES/sec

Memory
Up to 16 shared memory modules of
64 or 256 MBYTES each (4 GBYTES)

Memory Bus Bandwidth
640 MBYTES/sec

Software Environment
Operating system: Concentrix (Berkeley
4.3 UNIX compatible with parallel
extensions)
Programming Languages:
FX/FORTRAN with 8X extensions,
FX/Ada, FX/C

Network Services
Ethernet, TCP/IP, DECnet, NFS, NCS,
NQS, UltraNet, FDDI, HIPPI

Information Confirmed
21 November 1991
Alliant Computer Systems Corporation
One Monarach Drive
Littleton, MA 01460
Phone 508-486-1329
Fax 508-486-1329
Jay Maguire
Senior Sales Representative

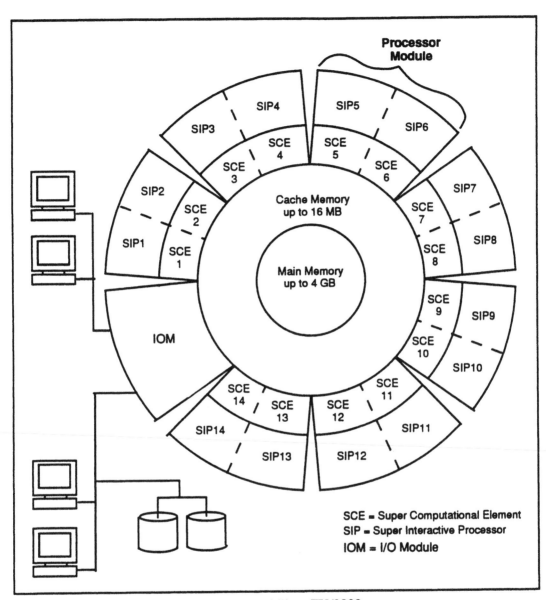

Figure A-1. Alliant FX/2800

Active Memory Technology DAP 610C

System Type
SIMD

Topology
Distributed memory, four-way nearest neighbor connectivity and row and column data paths

Processor Type
1 bit processor with 8 bit coprocessor

Cycle Time (Clock Rate)
100 nsec (10 MHz)

Peak Speed
40 Billion 1 bit logical operations per sec
20 Billion 8-bit integer adds per sec
560 MFLOPS 32 bit additions
408 MFLOPS 32 bit multiplications

Number of Processors
4,096 (4K)

Memory
4-128 KBYTES/processor
(16-512 MBYTES total)

Memory-to-Processor Bandwidth
5.1 GBYTES/sec 1 bit processor
40 GBYTES/sec 8 bit coprocessor

Processor-to-Processor Bandwidth
5.1 GBYTES/sec (nearest neighbor)
5.1 GBYTES/sec (row/column broadcast)
If information is to be sent to a subset of the processors, a global mask must be broadcast before the information is broadcast.

I/O Bandwidth
100 MBYTES/sec (consumes less than 3% of memory bandwidth)

Software Environment
Host systems: Sun Systems and VAX
Operating systems: UNIX, VAX/VMS
Programming Languages: FORTRAN*,
APAL assembler

Applications Packages
Image processing library, digital signal processing library, interactive debugging system, graphics library, general purpose math library, PDT parallel data transforms library

Information Confirmed
18 November 1991
Active Memory Technology, Inc. (AMT)
525 Bridgeport Avenue, Suite 105
Shelton, CT 06484
Phone 203-925-1075
16802 Aston Street, Suite 103
Irvine, CA 92714
Thomas J. Massage
North East Regional Sales Manager

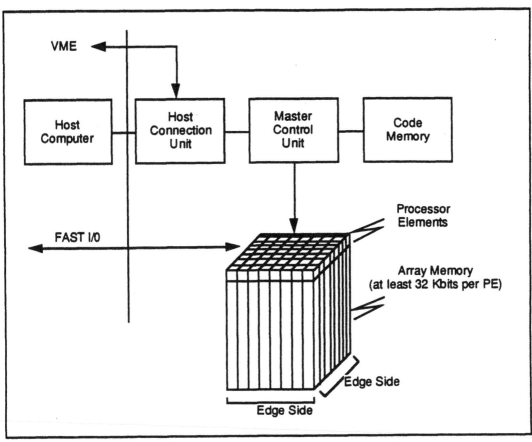

Figure A-2. Active Memory Technology DAP 610

BBN TC2000 Multiprocessor

System Type
MIMD

Topology
Globally addressable distributed memory,
butterfly switch

Processor Type
Motorola 88100 RISC processor with
floating point pipelines

Cycle Time (Clock Rate)
50 nsec (20 MHz)

Peak Speed
13 Whetstone MIPS/processor,
20 MFLOPS/processor,
34000 Dhrystones/processor

Number of Processors
8 - 128 (designed to support 512)

Processor Cache
32 KBYTES/processor instruction cache,
64 KBYTES/processor data cache

Memory
4 - 16 MBYTES/processor

Memory-to-Processor Bandwidth
Local access 80 MBYTES/sec,
Remote access 38 MBYTES/sec per path

Software Environment
Operating systems: nX (Berkeley UNIX
4.3 compatible). Also supports pSOS+m
Real-Time executive and the X Window
system.
Programming Languages: FORTRAN,
C, and Ada with BBN parallel
extensions, C++
Development Tools: Xtra Tool Set
includes the TotalView parallel
debugger and the GIST performance
analysis tool

Network Services
Ethernet, TCP/IP, NFS, DDN

Information Confirmed
21 November 1991
BBN Advanced Computers, Inc.
10 Fawcett Street
Cambridge, MA 02138
Phone 617-873-3457/3786
Fax 617-873-3315
Tom Blackadar
Director, Operations

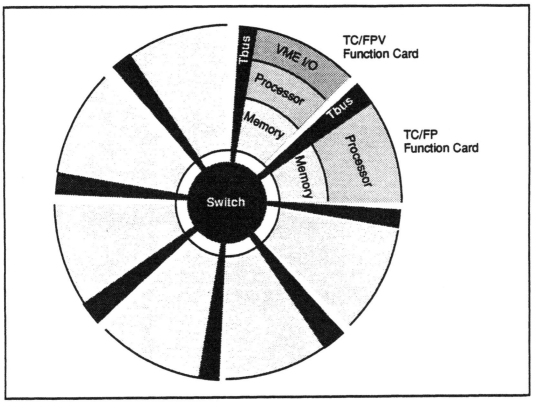

Figure A-3a. BBN TC2000 Architecture

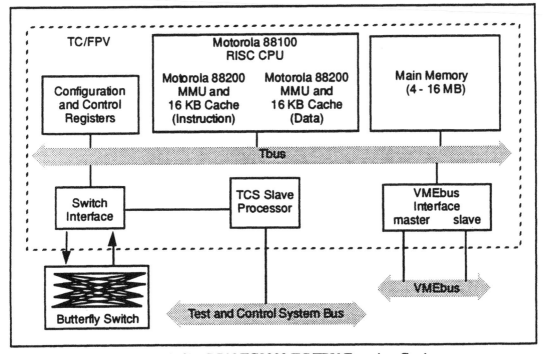

Figure A-3b. BBN TC2000 TC/FPV Function Card

Cogent Research XTM Series

System Type
MIMD

Topology
Processors connected by 32-bit parallel
bus and four 32 by 32 crossbar switches.
The four crossbar switch allow as many
as four processors to be connected to the
same processor at the same time.

Processor Type
Inmos T800

Cycle Time (Clock Rate)
33 nsec (30 MHz)

Peak Speed
132 MFLOPS, 940 MIPS

Number of Processors
2 - 32

Memory
488 MBYTES

Processor-to-Processor Bandwidth
32-bit parallel bus (LindaBus)
40 MBYTES/sec;
transputer links 20 MBITS/sec

Software Environment
Operating system: QIX, a parallel
operating system with Kernel Linda;
compatible with UNIX
Programming Languages: FORTRAN,
C, C++, Linda parallel extensions, Lisp
Development Tools: PIX PostScript and
NeWS compatible window system,
X Windows, program monitoring and
debugging tools

Network Services
Ethernet, TCP/IP

Information Confirmed
19 November 1991
Cogent Research Incorporated
1100 NW Compton Drive
Beaverton, Oregon 97006-6998
Phone 503-690-1450
Fax 503-690-1344
Jeffrey Lang

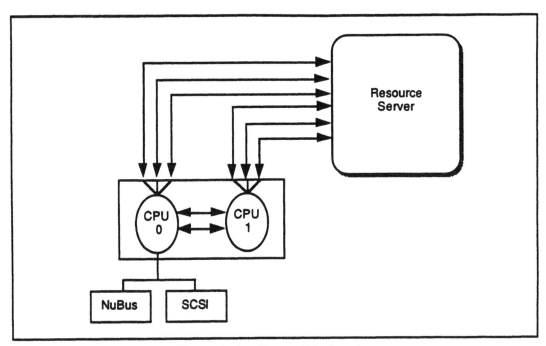

Figure A-4a. Cogent Workstation

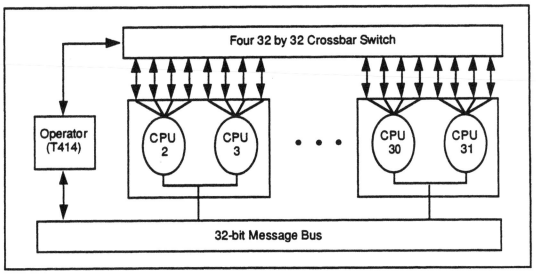

Figure A-4b. Cogent Resource Server

CONVEX C38 Series

System Type
MIMD

Topology
Shared-memory, crossbar switch

Processor Type
ECL/CMOS 64-bit integrated
scalar/vector/symmetric parallel
processor

Cycle Time (Clock Rate)
16 nsec (62 MHz)

Peak Speed
125 MFLOPS/processor 64-bit,
250 MFLOPS/processor 32-bit

Number of Processors
1-8

Processor Cache
4 KBYTE scalar instruction cache (cache
is bypassed for vector operations)

Memory
256-4,096 MBYTES

Memory-to-Processor Bandwidth
480 MBYTES/sec/processor

Software Environment
Operating systems: CONVEX UNIX,
an extended version of UNIX 4.3 BSD;
virtual memory and demand paging
supported. Also available is COVUE, a
software package that emulates the
VAX/VMS environment, POSIX
compliant.
Programming Languages: ANSI
standard FORTRAN 77, FORTRAN 77
with FORTRAN 90 array notations, C,
Ada, and C++. Compilers automatically
parallelize, vectorize, and globally
optimize the code.
Development Tools: multitasking
compilers, CXpa, performance analyzer,
CXdb X-Window-based debugger,
application compiler with
interprocedural analyzer/optimizer, and
AVS an application visualization system.

Applications Packages
Over 1100 third party libraries available
and are listed in the CONVEX ATLAS
catalogue.

Network Services
Supports industry-standard protocols,
including NFS, NCS, TCP/IP and
DECnet, HIPPI

Information Confirmed
25 November 1991
Corporate Headquarters:
CONVEX Computer Corporation
3000 Waterview Parkway
P.O. Box 833851
Richardson, TX 75083-3851
Local contact:
CONVEX Computer Corporation
6650 Collamer Road
E. Syracuse, NY 13057
Phone 315-463-7189
Fax 315-437-8283
Anthony DiMento
Account Executive

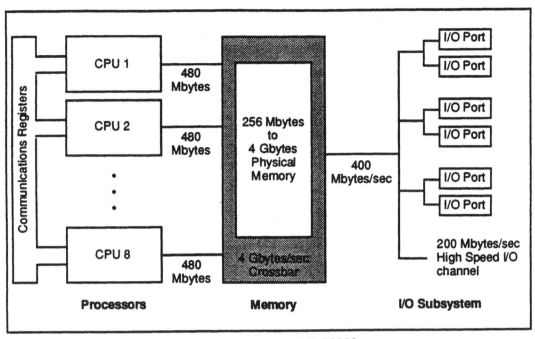

Figure A-5. CONVEX C3880

Cray Y-MP C90

System Type
MIMD

Topology
Shared-memory, bus-based

Processor Type
Dual pipelined vector processor

Cycle Time (Clock Rate)
4 nsec (250 MHz)

Peak Speed
1 GFLOPS/processor

Number of Processors
1 - 16

Memory
256 MEGAWORDS (1 word = 8 bytes)

Memory-to-Processor Bandwidth
250 GBYTES/sec

Software Environment
Operating system: UNICOS, based on
AT&T UNIX System V operating
system (full POSIX compliant), COS
Programming Languages:
FORTRAN 77 and ANSI C with
automatic vectorizing and multi-tasking,
FORTRAN D, C++, Pascal, Cray Ada,
Common Lisp, and SIMSCRIPT
(1993 FORTRAN 90)
Development Tools: X Windows,
debugging aids and performance
analysis tools for CPU and I/O, Cray
visualization toolkit, Motif, DGL
(Distributed Graphics Language), X
View, AVS, Explorer, Khoros (image
and signal processing library), Gipsy
(interactive image processing system),
VAST (FORTRAN compiler aid),
FORGE (FORTRAN 77 to FORTRAN
90 translator).

Network Services
TCP/IP, NFS, and Cray Research Station
Software protocols for proprietary
systems, HIPPI, FDDI, Ethernet, POSIX,
VME, Hyperchannel, RAID (external
disk array), ESDI

Information Confirmed
22 November 1991
Cray Research, Inc.
1900 West Park Drive
Suite 420
Westborough, MA 01581
Phone 508-898-2531
Fax 508-366-4359
1-800-284-2729
Mardi Schmieder
Corporate Communications

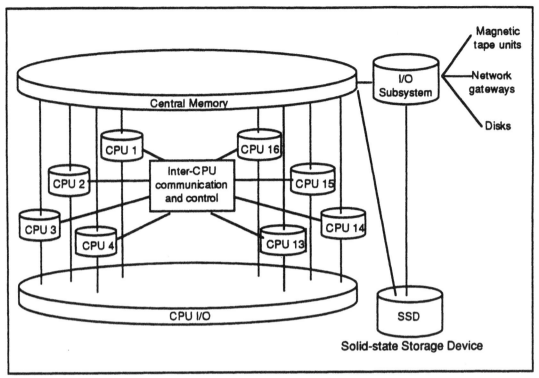

Figure A-6. Cray Y-MP Series

Encore Multimax 520

System Type
MIMD

Topology
Shared-memory, bus-based

Processor Type
National Semiconductor NS32532
microprocessor

Cycle Time (Clock Rate)
33 nsec (30 MHz)

Peak Speed
170 MIPS (8.5 MIPS/processor)

Number of Processors
2 - 20

Memory
32 - 640 MBYTES

Memory-to-Processor Bandwidth
100 MBYTES/sec

Software Environment
Operating systems: UMAX 4.3 (UNIX
4.3 compatible), UMAX V (UNIX
System V compatible) and MACH.
Programming Languages: Encore
Parallel FORTRAN, Ada, C, Pascal,
Lisp, BASIC, and COBOL.

Network Services
TCP/IP, NFS, X.25, and other standards

Information Confirmed
15 August 1990
Encore Computer Corporation
Eastern Operations
257 Cedar Hill Street
Marlborough, MA 01752-3089
Phone 508-485-0709
Fax 508-485-0709
Richard A. DiMarzo
Regional Manager

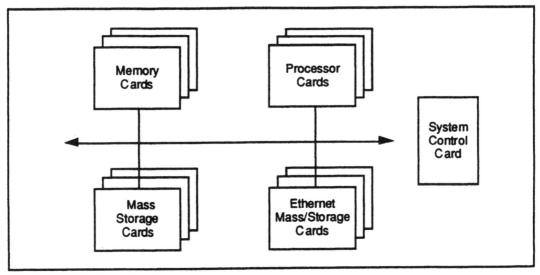

Figure A-7. Encore Multimax System Architecture

IBM ES/9000 Model 900

System Type
MIMD

Topology
Processors directly linked via fiber optic channels to dual control elements which contain 2 MBYTE high-speed buffers. Shared memory system is partitionable, either physically, logically, or in software

Processor Type
Proprietary processor with Vector Facility (VF) provides eight 64-bit vector registers or sixteen 32-bit vector registers, with 256 data elements in each register

Cycle Time (Clock Rate)
9 nsec (110 MHz)

Peak Speed
444 MFLOPS/processor

Number of Processors
Up to 6 processors with up to 6 VFs

Processor Cache
128 KBYTES data buffer and 128 KBYTES instruction buffer/processor allows concurrent instruction and data fetches

Memory
1024 MBYTES central storage, 8192 MBYTES expanded storage 16 TERABYTE virtual address space. Expanded storage can be used for paging. 4 K page can be moved between expanded storage and central storage in less than 25 microseconds.

Memory-to-Processor Bandwidth
Extended store to CPU and central store to CPU transfer rates are not published

Software Environment
Operating systems: MVS/ESA (Extended System Architecture), VM/ESA, AIX/ESA (UNIX-based), VSE, DPPX (Distributed Processing Programming Executive). Virtual memory, Operating systems compatible with earlier architectures
Programming Languages: VS FORTRAN (supports explicit fork and join) and APL2 both with automatic vectorization, C, Pascal and Ada/370. FORTRAN-90 will be supported eventually.
Development Tools: Optimization Subroutine Library (OSL), Data Facility Storage Management Subsystem (DFSMS), Dynamic Reconfiguration Management (DRM). Supports the Engineering and Scientific Subroutine Library (ESSL), X Windows, 700 third party applications

Network Services
IBM NetView supports SNA, TCP/IP, OSI, DECnet, Ethernet, Ultranet (which supports VME), FDDI, HIPPI. Through HIPPI fiber (rather than copper) I/O channels, one in one out (rather than copper), provides 17 MBYTES/sec.

Additional Options
Sysplex Timer

Information Confirmed
11 June 1992
International Business Machines
Gene Hozafel, Scientific Marketing Group
301-564-2095

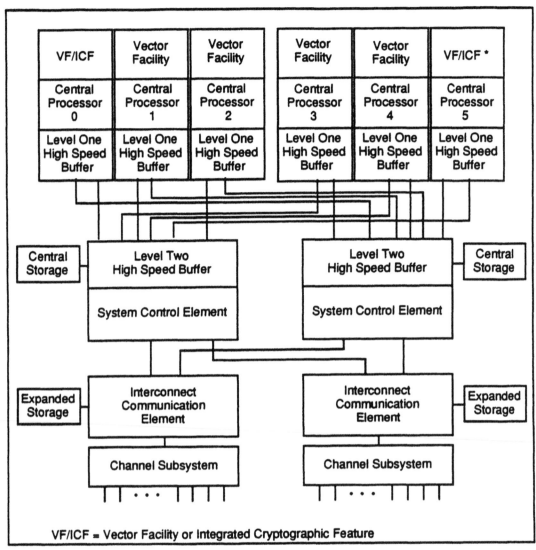

Figure A-8. IBM ES/9000 Model 900

Intel iPSC/860

System Type
MIMD

Topology
Distributed-memory, hypercube

Processor Type
i860 RISC microprocessor

Cycle Time (Clock Rate)
25 nsec (40 MHz)

Peak Speed
33 MIPS, 80 single/60 double precision
MFLOPS/processor

Number of Processors
8 - 128

Memory
64 - 2048 MBYTES

Processor-to-Processor Bandwidth
2.8 MBYTES/sec

I/O Facilities
Concurrent File System (CFS), a
UNIX-like system with automatic disk-
striping

Software Environment
Host systems: Intel 386 platform, or
SUN remote hosts
Operating systems: UNIX System V
release 3.2 on host and NX/2 kernel
operating system on processors
Programming Languages: FORTRAN,
C
Development Tools: IPD parallel
debugger; FORGE, for parallelizing
large FORTRAN programs; PAT, a
Performance Analysis Tool; ProSolvers,
a Parallel Matrix Solutions Library;
DGL, Distributed Graphics Library,
X Windows

Network Services
TCP/IP, FTP, Ethernet, NFS, NQS

Information Confirmed
13 December 1991
INTEL Scientific Computers
15201 N. W. Greenbrier Parkway
Beaverton, Oregon 97006
Phone 503-629-7600
Steve Cannon
Product Manager

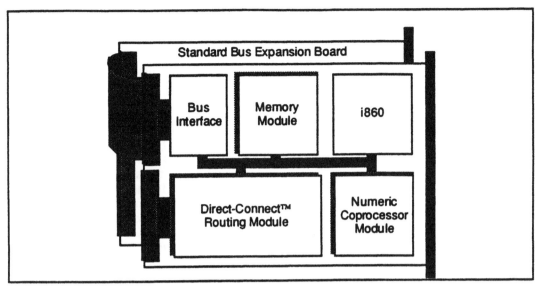

Figure A-9. iPSC Node Board

Intel Paragon XP/S

Paragon available fourth quarter of 1992
based on Touchstone Sigma Machine

System Type
MIMD

Topology
2D mesh of node boards, each node
board has 1 application processor
(Late 1993: 4 processors sharing
64-MBYTES of memory)

Processor Type
i860-XP

Cycle Time (Clock Rate)
20 nsec (50 MHz)

Processor Cache
16 KBYTES internal cache

Peak Speed
42 MIPS/processor
75 MFLOPS/processor double precision

Number of Processors
66 to 1024 nodes
(Late 1993 4 processors/node)

Memory
16-32 MBYTES/node
Late 1993
16-64 MBYTES memory shared among
4 processors
256 KBYTES cache/processor
Early 1994
16-128 MBYTES /node

Processor-to-Processor Bandwidth
200 MBYTES/sec
25 microsec latency end-to-end

Software Environment
Operating systems: OSF UNIX with
Mach Kernel
Programming Languages: FORTRAN,
C, Ada, C++, Data-parallel FORTRAN,
FORTRAN-90 (late 1992)
Development Tools: , X Windows, IPD
parallel debugger; FORGE and CAST
parallelization tools; iPVS Hardware-
aided Intel Performance Visualization
System, Intel ProSolver parallel equation
solver, math libraries, Motif, DGL
(Distributed Graphics Language allows
rendering on workstation—data is sent to
workstation as graphics commands
rather than pixels)
Working with DEC on High
Performance FORTRAN automatic data-
parallelism tool (Early 1993)

Network Services
TCP/IP, FTP, Ethernet, NFS, HIPPI,
Unitree file manager

Information Confirmed
26 May 1992
INTEL Scientific Computers
15201 N. W. Greenbrier Parkway
Beaverton, Oregon 97006
Phone 503-629-7600
Steve Cannon
Product Manager

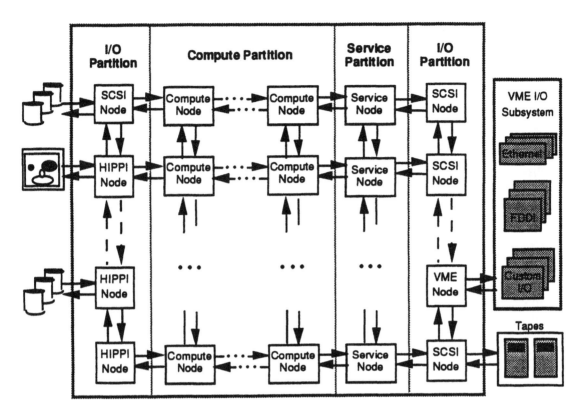

Figure A-10. Intel Paragon System Architecture

Kendell Square Research KSR-1

System Type
MIMD

Topology
Distributed caches connected by a
hierarchical search engine. Data moves
to the point of reference.

Processor Type
Proprietary RISC superscalar 64-bit;
64-bit addressing (top 24 bits zero on
KSR1)

Cycle Time (Clock Rate)
50 nsec (20 MHz)

Peak Speed
40 MFLOPS/processor,
40 MIPS/processor

Number of Processors
8-1088

Processor Cache
256 KBYTES/processor instruction cache,
256 KBYTES/processor data cache

Memory
512 KBYTES subcache/node
32 MBYTES cache/node
1 TBYTE/process of virtual memory

Memory-to-Processor Bandwidth
Subcache: 160 MBYTES/sec
Local cache: 50 MBYTES/sec
Remote search group 0:
1 GBYTES/sec
Remote search group 1:
1 GBYTES/sec per path
4 GBYTES/sec aggregate

I/O Bandwidth
210 - 15,300 MBYTES/sec

Software Environment
Operating systems: UNIX (OSF/1
compatible)
Programming Languages: COBAL,
FORTRAN, C automatic and
semiautomatic parallelization with
directives using Presto parallel run-time
environment.
Development Tools: X Windows, Motif,
NFS, dbx compatible parallel debugger,
KSR parallel performance analysis tool
Applications: ORACLE DBMS

Network Services
TCP/IP, Ethernet, SNA, ISO/OSI, FDDI,
HIPPI, VME

Information Confirmed
April 1992
Steve Frank
Kendell Square Research
170 Tracer Lane
Waltham, MA 02154-1379
Phone 617-895-9400
6401 Golden Triangle Dr. Suite 450
Greenbelt, Maryland 20770
301-220-1396

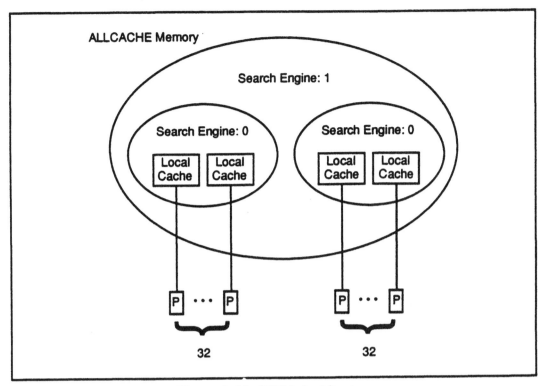

Figure A-11. KSR1 Architecture

MasPar 1200

System Type
SIMD

Topology
Distributed memory, 2-dimensional array of processors terroidally wrapped at edges. X-Net, 8-way nearest neighbor communications and Global router communications.

Processor Type
Proprietary four bit serial processor

Cycle Time (Clock Rate)
80 nsec (12 MHz)

Peak Speed
1.2 GFLOPS (0.075 MFLOPS/processor) 32-bit,
550 MFLOPS (0.034 MFLOPS/processor) 64-bit,
26,000 MIPS (1.6 MIPS/processor)
or 0.2 32-bit MIPS/processor)

Number of Processors
1024 - 16,384 (1K - 16K)

Processor Cache
192 BYTES on chip static RAM

Memory
16 or 64 KBYTES DRAM per PE

Memory-to-Processor Bandwidth
100 GBYTES/sec

Processor-to-Processor Bandwidth
18 GBYTES/sec (nearest neighbor)
1.3 GBYTES/sec (global)

Software Environment
Host system: VAXstation DS 5000/2000
Operating system: UNIX
Programming Languages: MasPar FORTRAN, FORTRAN-90, MasPar Parallel Application Language
Development Tools: X Windows, symbolic debugger, interactive profiler, performance visualization tool, VAST-2 FORTRAN 77 to MasPar FORTRAN translator, Mathematics and Image Processing Libraries

Network Services
Ethernet, TCP/IP, NFS, HIPPI (1993)

Information Confirmed
19 November 1991
MasPar Computer Corporation
945 Concord Avenue
Framingham, MA 01701
508-879-9242
Fax 508-879-0698
George Themaras
North Eastern Manager

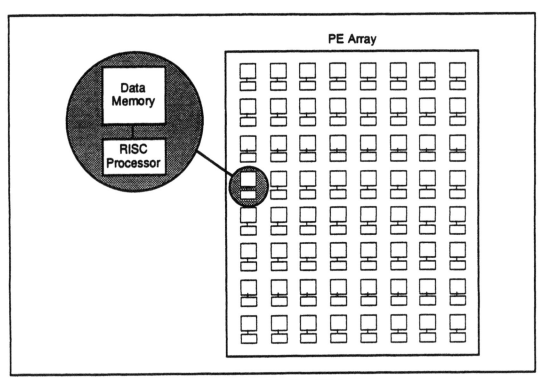

Figure A-12a. MasPar PE Array

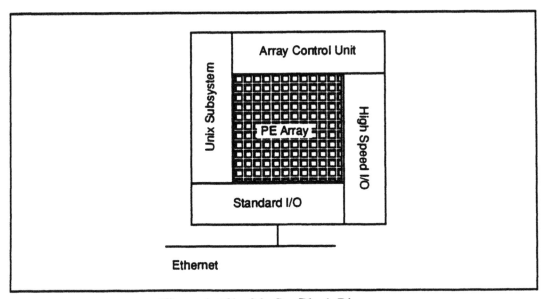

Figure A-12b. MasPar Block Diagram

Meiko Computing Surface

System Type
MIMD

Topology
Distributed memory, reconfigureable
topology

Processor Type
Intel i860

Cycle Time (Clock Rate)
25 nsec (40 MHz)

Peak Speed
80 MFLOPS/processor, 40 MIPS/processor

Number of Processors
2 - 700

Memory
8-32 MBYTES/processor

Processor-to-Processor Bandwidth
6 MBYTES/sec

Software Environment
Operating system: SUNOS 4.1.1,
CS-Tools
Host system: Sun workstation
Programming Languages: C,
FORTRAN 77, Pascal, Occam,
Modula 2, C++

Network Services
Ethernet, TCP/IP, NFS

Information Confirmed
February 1992
Meiko Scientific Corporation
Reservoir Place
1601 Trapelo Road
Waltham, MA 02154
Phone 617-890-7676
Fax 617-890-5042
1555 Wilson Blvd. Suite 300
Arlington, VA 22209
Phone 703-875-8710
Marc Cotnoir

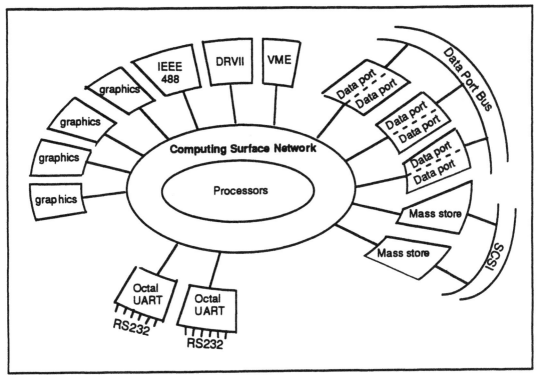

Figure A-13. Meiko Computing Surface

Myrias SPS-3

System Type
MIMD

Topology
Globally addressable distributed memory,
bus hierarchy

Processor Type
Motorola MC68040 microprocessor

Cycle Time (Clock Rate)
40 nsec (25 MHz)

Peak Speed
8.3 MFLOPS/processor,
25 MIPS/processor

Number of Processors
16 - 4096 or more

Processor Cache
16 KBYTES/processor instruction cache,
16 KBYTES/processor data cache

Memory
8-16 MBYTES/processor

Memory-to-Processor Bandwidth
Local access: 50 - 100 MBYTES/sec
Remote access:
33 MBYTES/sec per intercage link,
627 MBYTES/sec per cage

Software Environment
Host system: SPARC-based
Operating systems: UNIX-like (POSIX)
with automatic load balancing
(demonstrated on 1044 processors-
system overhead increases
logarithmically with the number of
processors)
Programming Languages: Myrias
Parallel FORTRAN, C (can do code
block, subroutine, or loop-level
parallelization)
Development Tools: Myrias Parallel
Debugger, Mprof, Xmtask and Xmperf
performance analysis tools, X Windows

Network Services
Ethernet, NFS, TCP/IP, and standard
Sun network software

Information Confirmed
December 1991
Myrias Computer Technologies Inc.
8522 Davies Road
Edmondton, Alberta, Canada T6E 4Y5
(313) 625-4381
Wayne T. Karpoff

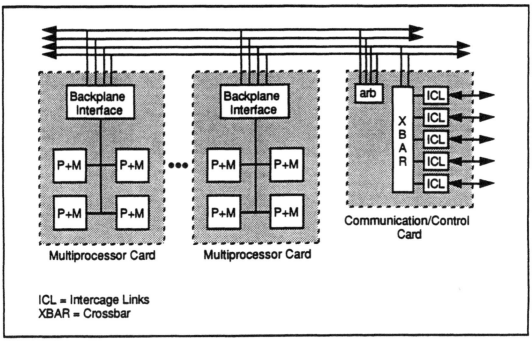

Figure A-14. Myrias SPS-3

NCUBE 2

System Type
MIMD

Topology
Distributed memory, hypercube

Processor Type
Proprietary VLSI design 64-bit
processor

Cycle Time (Clock Rate)
50 nsec (20 MHz)

Peak Speed
7.5 MIPS
3.3 MFLOPS/processor

Number of Processors
8 - 8192

Processor Cache
128 BYTES instruction cache

Memory
1 - 16 MBYTES/processor

Processor-to-Processor Bandwidth
2.2 MBYTES/sec per DMA channel,
100 microsec latency

Software Environment
Host systems: Sun Workstation, VAX
mini-computer, Silicon Graphics
Operating systems: Parallel AT&T
System 5.3 UNIX
Programming Languages:
FORTRAN 77, C, C++
Development Tools: Ndb (a parallel
debugger), profiler

Applications Packages
Extensive math library, ORACLE
RDBMS, hundreds of third party
compute-intensive scientific and
business applications

Network Services
Ethernet, NFS, TCP/IP, HIPPI (1993)

Information Confirmed
9 December 1991
NCUBE
919 East Hillside Blvd.
Foster City, CA 94404
415-593-9000
800-35-NCUBE or 800-654-2823
Wendy Allen
Assistant Director, Corporate
Communications

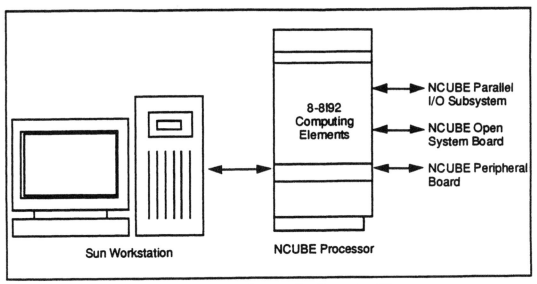

Figure A-15. NCUBE System Configuration Diagram

NEC SX-3 Model 44R

System Type
MIMD

Topology
Shared-memory, bus-based

Processor Type
RISC processors with vector and scalar
pipelines (each processor contains
4 pipeline sets)

Cycle Time (Clock Rate)
2.5 nsec (400 MHz)

Peak Speed
25.6 GFLOPS, 789 MIPS

Number of Processors
4

Memory
128 MBYTES - 8 GBYTES

Memory-to-Processor Bandwidth
Transfer rates are not published

Software Environment
Operating system: SUPER-UX (UNIX
System V compatible)
Programming Languages:
FORTRAN 77/SX and C with automatic
vectorization and parallelization
capabilities
Development Tools: CONVERTER/SX
converts FORTRAN programs from
other supercomputers to the SX-3 Series

Network Services
Hyperchannel, Ethernet, Telnet, TCP/IP,
NFS, NQS, UNIX STREAMS

Information Confirmed
20 December 1991
HNSX Supercomputers, Inc.
77 South Bedford Street
Burlington, MA 01803
Phone 617-270-7600
Samuel W. Adams
Vice President of Marketing Operations

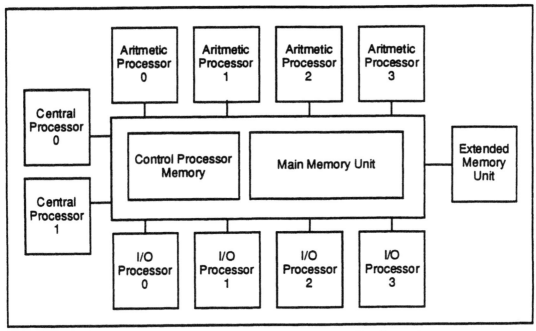

Figure A-16. NEC SX-3 R-Series System Configuration

Sequent Symmetry 2000/750

System Type
MIMD

Topology
Bus-based, shared-memory

Processor Type
Intel 486

Cycle Time (Clock Rate)
20 nsec (50 MHz)

Peak Speed
420 MIPS

Number of Processor
2 - 30

Processor Cache
512 KBYTES/processor

Memory
8 - 832 MBYTES

Storage
Dual Channel Disk Controllers (DCC's)
support up to 56 disks (84 GBYTES of
storage)

Memory-to-Processor Bandwidth
80 MBYTES/sec

Software Environment
Operating system: DYNIX/PPX
(enhanced UNIX System 5.3)
Programming Languages:
FORTRAN 77, C, Pascal, ANSI
COBOL
Development Tools:_DYNIX Monitor,
Performance tools within database
environment

Applications Packages
Third party software, Database
application environment, X Windows

Network Services
Ethernet, TCP/IP, NFS, X.25, IBM
SNA, Bisync, Novell, VME

Information Confirmed
21 November 1991
Sequent Computer Systems, Inc.
15450 S. W. Koll Parkway
Beaverton, OR 97006-6063
Phone 1-800-854-0428
Ron Parsons
Manager, Technical Marketing

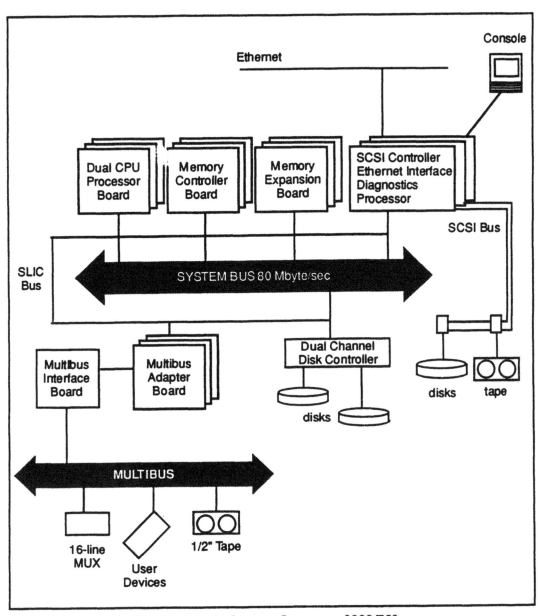

Figure A-17. Sequent Symmetry 2000/750

Thinking Machines CM-2

System Type
SIMD

Topology
Distributed memory, nearest neighbor,
16 processors and local memory are
contained on one chip and arranged in a
12-dimensional hypercube.

Processor Type
Bit-serial

Cycle Time (Clock Rate)
125 nsec (8 MHz)

Peak Speed
4000 MIPS (8-bit byte add)
2500 MIPS (32-bit integer add)
31 GFLOPS

Number of Processors
65,536

Memory
2 GBYTES

Data Vault
Mass storage system holds 10-20
GBYTES and sustains 25 MBYTES/sec
transfer

Memory-to-Processor Bandwidth
3 GBITS/sec

Processor-to-Processor Bandwidth
Information not published

Software Environment
Host systems: Sun-4 or VAX 6300
running UNIX or Symbolics 3600-series
Lisp Machine
Operating systems: Computer uses the
operating system of the host machine.
Programming Languages:
CM-FORTRAN, C*, *Lisp

Applications Packages
Include numerous fundamental physics
simulations, wind-tunnel simulation, ray-
tracing, hydrodynamic modeling,
seismic data processing, helicopter wake
simulation

Information Unconfirmed
Thinking Machines Corporation
245 First Street
Cambridge, MA 02142-1214
Phone 617-876-1111
Tim Browne
Director of Communications

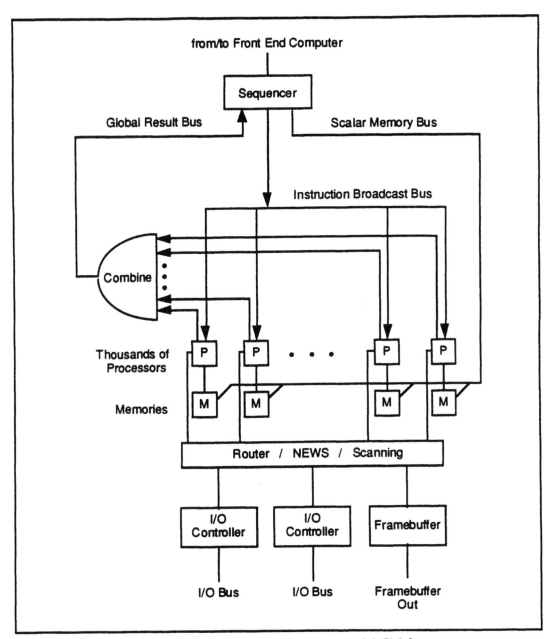

Figure A-18 Thinking Machines Model CM-2

Thinking Machines CM-5

System Type
SPMD (Single Program Multiple Data)
The same program is loaded on every
node of a partition. A partition contains
32 or more processing nodes and a
control processor (a Sun workstation).
Each node executes the program
asynchronously.

Topology
Distributed memory, fat-tree
connectivity; data and synchronization
control network

Processor Type
22 MIPS SPARC RISC microprocessor
each with four 64-bit vector units; vector
units support floating point, integer, and
logical operations.

Cycle Time (Clock Rate)
30 nsec (33 MHz)

Peak Speed
128 MFLOPS/processor,
128 MIPS/processor

Number of Processors
32-16K

Memory
32 MBYTES/node

Processor-to-Processor Bandwidth
5 MBYTES/sec per pair of processors
simultaneously for all pairs of nodes.
30-MBYTES/sec between nearest
neighbors
2 - 4 microsecs latency for data network
1 - 2 microsecs latency for control
(synchronization) network

Software Environment
Operating systems: CMost (enhanced
version of UNIX); virtual memory and
multiple users are supported. Each node
contains an operating system micro-
kernel, each partition contains a full
operating system.
Programming Languages:
CM-FORTRAN, FORTRAN 90, C*,
*Lisp
Development Tools: Prism (Motif based
software development environment:
debugger, performance monitor, data
visualization), AVS (Automatic
Visualization System), Explorer,
CMX11 (X Windows), CMSSL
(Scientific Software Library), CMMD
(message-passing library for host/node
programming), NQS (Network Queuing
System job batching system with
automatic check-pointing).

I/O
Scalable disk-array comes in 25 GBYTES
units; each unit has 33 MBYTES/sec
aggregate transfer rate.

Network Services
Ethernet, NFS, FDDI, HIPPI,VME,
TCP/IP, Ultranet

Information Unconfirmed
June 2, 1992
Thinking Machines Corporation
245 First Street
Cambridge, MA 02142-1214
Phone 617-876-1111
Jim Reardon
Sales Manager

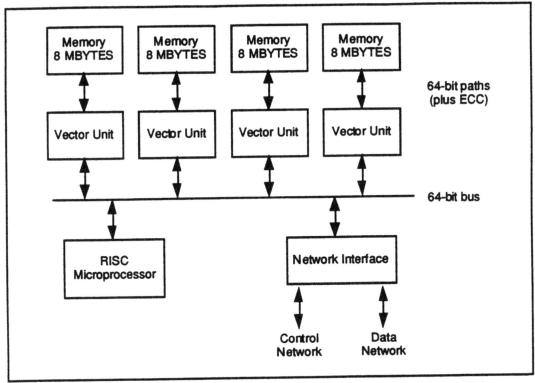

Figure A-19a. Thinking Machines CM-5 Processing Node with Vector Units

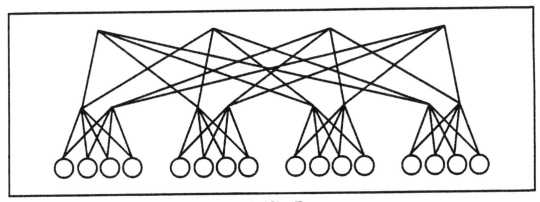

Figure A-19b. Fat-tree

Table A-1. Characteristics of Individual Machines

	Architecture Type		Memory			Interconnect Topology					Maximum Number of Processors		
	SIMD	MIMD	Shared	Distributed	Hybrid	Bus	Mesh	Hypercube	Switch	Other	< 32	32 - 1024	> 1024
Alliant FX/2800		X	X			X					X		
AMT DAP 610C	X			X			X			X			X
BBN TC2000		X			X				X			X	
Cogent XTM		X		X		X			X		X		
CONVEX C3		X	X						X		X		
CRAY Y-MP		X	X			X					X		
Encore 520		X	X			X					X		
IBM ES/9000 900		X	X			X					X		
Intel IPSC/860		X		X				X				X	
Intel Paragon		X		X			X					X	
KSR-1		X			X					X		X	
MasPar MP-1	X			X			X			X			X
Melko		X		X						X		X	
Myrias SPS-3		X			X					X			X
NCUBE 2		X		X				X					X
NEC SX-3 44		X	X			X					X		
Sequent 2000/750		X	X			X					X		
TM CM-2	X			X			X	X					X
TM CM-5		X		X			X	X		X			X

APPENDIX B

GLOSSARY OF TERMS AND ABBREVIATIONS

Provided below are the major terms and abbreviations that are found in this document and that are used throughout literature on high-performance computers.

Annotations: Compiler directives.

ANSI: Computer language standards maintained by the American National Standard Institute, Inc.

Barrier Synchronization: A method for synchronizing processors in which each processor is delayed at a specific barrier point in a program until all processors have reached that point.

Bottleneck: Usually a pileup of processes caused by a resource that cannot keep up.

BSD: Berkeley Standard for the UNIX operating system.

Byte: Eight bits of data.

Cache: A small-capacity, high-speed buffer memory used to provide an effective reduction of main memory access times.

Cache Coherence: The requirement that each cache in a multiple processor system have the same value for any shared memory location.

Cluster: A style of configuring multiple processors by connecting them to a common external communications circuit.

Coarse-Grain Parallelism: Computation in which the unit of computation is large compared to communication costs and other system overheads.

Concurrency: Parallelism.

Contention: Completion of processes for the use of a resource, usually causing performance degradation.

Critical Section: A section of a program which is to be executed by only one process at a time.

Crossbar: An interconnection in which each input is connected to each output through a single switch.

Cycle Time: CPU access time to primary storage.

DARPA: U. S. Department of Defense Advanced Research Projects Agency.

Data Flow: The sequence of operations that are performed on a collection of data during a computation.

Data Flow Computer : A computer in which the order of computation is determined by the availability of the required data.

Deadlock: A condition in which two or more processes cannot proceed because each is either directly or indirectly waiting for the other.

Dependency Analysis: An analysis showing which parts of a program depend on the prior completion of other parts.

Disk Striping: A software mechanism which divides data into blocks and distributes it across multiple disks, so that multiple reads and writes can be performed in parallel.

Distributed Memory: A memory architecture in which each processor has its own local memory.

DRAM: Dynamic random access memory.

Efficiency: The average utilization of the processors allocated for a program.

Elaboration: Elaboration of the declaration (in an Ada program) is the process by which a declaration achieves its effect. This process happens during program execution. After its elaboration, a declaration is said to be elaborated. The elaboration of a task body has no other effect than to establish that the body can from then on be used for the execution of tasks designated by objects of the corresponding task type. [DOD:83]

Fine-Grain Parallelism: Computation in which the unit of computation is small compared to communication costs and other system overheads.

FORTRAN 8x: The new standard FORTRAN which includes new constructs for processing arrays of data to allow for more efficient programming of vector and parallel computers.

GBYTES (Gigabytes): 1024^3 bytes (sometimes referred to as one billion bytes).

GFLOPS (Gigaflops): One billion floating point operations per second.

Granularity: A measure of the size of a unit of computation.

Hypercube: A parallel computer whose processors are connected as if they were corners of a multidimensional cube and the connections were the edges.

KBYTES (Kilobytes): 1024 bytes (sometimes referred to as one thousand bytes).

Kernel: The nucleus of an operating system. Resides in primary storage.

Latency: The delay between a request for data and when it is received.

LIW/VLIW (Long Instruction Word and Very Long Instruction Word): An architecture in which fine-grain parallelism is attained by packing many instructions in a single word and processing them concurrently.

Massively Parallel: Large number (greater than 1000) of processors, usually slower than other types of processors.

MBYTES (Megabytes): 1024^2 bytes (sometimes referred to as one million bytes).

MFLOPS (Megaflops): An execution rate measured in units of a million floating point operations per second.

MHz (Megahertz): One million cycles per second.

MIMD (Multiple Instruction Stream, Multiple Data Stream): According to Flynn's taxonomy, a method of parallel processing in which multiple processors can execute different instructions on different data simultaneously.

MIPS (Millions of Instructions per Second): An execution rate measured in units of million instructions per second.

Monitor: A shared data structure and set of functions that access the data structure to control the synchronization of concurrent processes.

Multiprocessor: A parallel computer comprising many independent processors and facilities for interconnecting them and controlling their interactions.

Mutual Exclusion: A sequence of statements that are treated atomically.

nsec (nanosecond): The unit of time which is equal to 10^{-9} second.

Object-Oriented Programming: A programming paradigm in which data and code are encapsulated in entities called objects which interact by the exchange of messages.

Parallel Computing: Programs that use multiple processors concurrently to carry out computations.

Pipeline: A hardware structure with a sequence of stages through which a computation proceeds and in which new operations can be initiated in assembly-line fashion.

Race condition: A set of circumstances in which the relative speeds of the processes lead to results that may be difficult to predict. This condition may exist when two or more threads of control participate in unsynchronized access to a common resource.

RAM: Random access memory.

RISC (Reduced Instruction Set Computer): A computer whose instruction set contains relatively few instructions—all of which are simple and require one or very few cycles to execute.

Scalability: Ability of a computer system to increase in size (with little redesign of its components) and still maintain efficiency.

Scalar Arithmetic: Arithmetic operations that manipulate individual pieces of data.

Semaphore: A protected synchronization variable whose value can be accessed and altered only by primitive, indivisible operations. A semaphore acts like a lock on a critical section of code, allowing only one process at a time to execute the code. Semaphores can be implemented in software or hardware.

Serialization: The forcing of a collection of tasks to be performed one at a time instead of in parallel.

Shared Memory: A memory architecture in which data can be accessed directly by all the processors.

SIMD (Single Instruction Stream, Multiple Data Stream): According to Flynn's taxonomy, a method of parallel processing in which multiple processors execute the same instruction on separate data elements simultaneously.

Speedup: The ratio of the time to execute a sequential program to the time to execute a parallel program for the same computation on a multiprocessor whose processing units are identical to the sequential processor.

Spinlock: A hardware or software shared variable that is continuously tested until a condition becomes true.

Supercomputer: A class of computer that represents the most powerful in existence. Supercomputers are grossly measured by floating point operations per second and are further differentiated from all other computers by price and application-processing capabilities.

Synchronization: The coordination of activity between processes or processors.

Tasking: Dividing a computer program into separate threads of control which may be performed concurrently.

Teraflops: One trillion floating point operations per second.

Vector : A data structure consisting of an ordered set of elements.

Vector Arithmetic: Arithmetic operations that manipulate vectors.

VLSI: Very Large Scale Integration

Von Neumann Computer: Computer that stores programs and data in memory and uses a program counter to control the execution of instructions.

Printed and bound by CPI Group (UK) Ltd, Croydon, CR0 4YY

03/10/2024

01040333-0011